State of Vermont
Department of Libraries
Midstate Regional Library
RFD #4
Montpelier, Vt. 05602

WITHDRAWN

Basketball for Young Champions

Robert J. Antonacci
and
Jene Barr

Illustrated
by
Patti Boyd

BASKETBALL for YOUNG CHAMPIONS

Second Edition

McGraw-Hill Book Company
New York   St. Louis   San Francisco   Auckland   Bogotá
Düsseldorf   Johannesburg   London   Madrid   Mexico
Montreal   New Delhi   Panama   Paris   São Paulo
Singapore   Sydney   Tokyo   Toronto

Other Books in the Young Champion Series

FOOTBALL FOR YOUNG CHAMPIONS, Second Edition
BASEBALL FOR YOUNG CHAMPIONS, Second Edition
PHYSICAL FITNESS FOR YOUNG CHAMPIONS, Second Edition
SOCCER FOR YOUNG CHAMPIONS
TRACK AND FIELD FOR YOUNG CHAMPIONS

Library of Congress Cataloging in Publication Data

Antonacci, Robert Joseph, date
  Basketball for young champions.

  (Young champion series)
  Includes index.
  SUMMARY: Presents a brief history of basketball and describes the fundamentals of the game, necessary skills, team play, and scoring.
  1. Basketball—Juvenile literature. [1. Basketball]
I. Barr, Jene, joint author. II. Boyd, Patti.
III. Title. IV. Series.
GV885.1.A57   1978   796.32'32   78-8029
ISBN 0-07-002141-4

Copyright © 1979 by Robert J. Antonacci and Jene Barr. All Rights Reserved. Printed in the United States of America. No part of this publication may be reproduced, stored in a retrieval system, or transmitted, in any form or by any means, electronic, mechanical, photocopying, recording, or otherwise, without the prior written permission of the publisher.

23456789 BPBP 7832109

CONTENTS

BASKETBALL—THE SPEEDY GAME	1
KNOW YOUR BASKETBALL	15
FOOTWORK IN BASKETBALL	25
HOW TO GUARD	32
DRIBBLING IN BASKETBALL	47
SHOOTING FOR BASKETS	59
PASSING IN BASKETBALL	77
CATCHING A BASKETBALL	91
SMART BASKETBALL	101
GETTING READY FOR THE BIG GAME	118
CAN YOU PASS THESE TESTS?	137
SCORES AND RECORDS	156
EVERYONE CAN PLAY BASKETBALL	169
DRIBBLE IT! PASS IT! SHOOT IT!	178
INDEX	180

Basketball for Young Champions

Chapter 1

Basketball— The Speedy Game

"All set?"

The referee stands at the center circle. He holds a basketball in his hands, a whistle at his lips. The two center players face each other inside the jump circle. Both teams are in their places, ready to go. It's the Panthers against the Wildcats!

Bright lights flood the playing court of the huge high-school gymnasium. Around the walls the stands are filled with boys and girls, men and women. They are basketball fans. Their eyes are on the referee.

The referee blows his whistle. He tosses the ball into the air. Up jump the centers. The game is on!

The tall Wildcat center taps the ball to his teammate Lightning Larry. Watch him! He charges down the court. Like the beat of a drum he dribbles the ball across the floor toward his basket.

Look! A scrappy Panther blocks Larry. In the stands the crowd wonders. What will Larry do? Will he pass? Will he try a long shot?

Without stopping, Larry bends down, whisks under the guard's arm, and keeps going.

The crowd yells, "Shoot! Larry! Shoot!"

As quick as lightning, Larry gets set and sinks a two-handed toss right into the basket!

This is modern basketball—the speedy game!

This exciting game is played by many people throughout the United States. Every city, town, and village has its basketball team. Boys and girls, men and women play this game in great numbers. And this popular game started with a couple of peach baskets and a soccer ball!

The Peach-basket Game

Back in 1891 there was no active game that young people could play indoors during the winter months.

Dr. James A. Naismith taught physical education at the YMCA Training School in Springfield, Massachusetts. He had an inventive mind. He took two peach baskets and fastened them on the balcony, one at each end of the school gymnasium. Then he had his students throw a soccer ball into the peach baskets. This was the beginning of basketball!

During the game a school janitor sat on top of a stepladder near each basket. Every time a player threw the ball into the basket, the janitor fished it out and dropped it down to the floor so that a new play could begin.

In time, the bottoms of the peach baskets were removed. Then the ball could drop right through to the floor. What an improvement! And the janitors were no longer needed.

Early Backboards and Baskets

The peach baskets gave way to wire mesh baskets. Then, in 1906, a metal hoop was used. But every time the ball missed the hoop, it fell into the crowd of spectators and everyone scrambled for it.

This slowed up the game, and it became clear that something had to be done to allow for better control of the ball. Another improvement was made. A backboard was put up behind the hoop. Now if a ball did not drop into the basket, it bounced against the backboard and fell down onto the playing field.

WOMEN'S UNIFORMS

1890's

1910–1915

Early Game Rules

In the early games seven men played on a team. Later, nine men were used, then eight, and finally five. And this number is used today.

Smith College is believed to have held the first women's basketball game in 1892. But the first official game rules for women were not adopted until 1899. At first they allowed nine players on a team, then six, and then five.

For many years the rules restricted women to playing on a specific area of the court. In 1967, a new rule was passed allowing women to play a full-court game like the men's game.

At one time, the game was divided into two periods of fifteen minutes each. Later, it was changed to three periods of twenty minutes each.

The ball was put into play by a "center jump" at the beginning of each half-period of play and after each field goal. If the ball went out of bounds, it belonged to the player who reached it first. The players could not walk or run with the ball. They had to stand and shoot, or pass the ball to a teammate. Dribbling was not allowed.

Early Scoring Rules

Every time the ball dropped into the basket, the scoring team received three points. When a team made three fouls, the opposing side received one point.

As time went on, the rule on fouls was changed. When a foul was made, the team fouled was allowed to let its best basket-shooter take a free throw.

Early Basketballs

Early basketball was played with a soccer ball, and for a short while with a Rugby football! But these balls did not work well because they were hard to control.

As more people began to play, the balls were improved. It wasn't until 1894 that a sports company produced the first real basketball for the inventor of the game. Rules were adopted that set the exact size and shape of the ball. The newer balls had more bounce and began to look like those we use today.

The game was now faster and more exciting. Later, the balls became more streamlined when they began to be made without laces. Even the name of the game, Basket Ball, was trimmed to one word, Basketball.

Early Uniforms

There were no definite uniforms for the early players. Some wore long pants and long-sleeved jerseys. Others wore track suits. Some even dressed up in their old-fashioned football uniforms.

Players wore long stockings, knee pads, and any kind of shoes they wished. In such uniforms they couldn't move very quickly.

For women players it was more difficult. At first they wore skirts made of layers of material. Some women players even wore long flannel trousers under the skirt. In 1912, they began to wear bloomers and a sailor's blouse.

About 1909, men's teams began to wear flannel or cotton basketball pants that reached down to the knees. These were a great improvement over the long pants and football uniforms. Then came shorter pants and short-sleeved jerseys. In 1914, a rule was passed, which stated that all players must wear numbers on the backs of their jerseys.

It's Played Outdoors!

In the spring of 1892, soon after the game was invented, a New York newspaper described a basketball game that was played outdoors. This game took place in New York City between a Student's Club team and a team from the YMCA. The Student's Club won by a score of 1—0! What a slow game that must have been!

During the nice weather people liked to play basketball outdoors. These outdoor games were played by "scrub" or "pick-up" teams. This means that teams picked up as many players as wanted to take part.

Sometimes outdoor playing courts had as many as one hundred players in a game, all scrambling after the ball. Fortunately, this kind of playing didn't last. The game continued to improve. People enjoyed watching and playing it. Today millions of people play some form of basketball in backyards, driveways, playgrounds, parks, picnic grounds, and even streets.

Basketball Teams Today

At the end of the playing season each year, America gets the "tournament fever." Teams get to work on their schedules. Game after game is played to find the championship teams. There are many classes of championships, ranging from those of young school teams to professionals.

Independent Team Championships

Many clubs and organizations sponsor their own championship tournaments. Thousands of players take part in these games. Factory and office workers, clerks, professional people, men, and women play on these teams. Everywhere, young boys and girls are active as members of their neighborhood teams. Great numbers of people watch these games and cheer for their teams. The end of each basketball season is always busy and exciting!

School Championship Games

Every city and town has its own school championship games. High-school teams play for the city and state championships. Most junior high schools and elementary schools also take part in tournaments to decide their own winning teams.

Wheelchair Basketball Competitions

Many sports events are sponsored for young players who have physical disabilities. Wheelchair basketball games are offered in neighborhoods, schools, and colleges. The *Wheelchair Basketball Association* sponsors competition in the *Para-Olympic Games*, which were first held in 1960 in Rome. Chapter Thirteen will tell you more about basketball for the physically handicapped player.

Special Olympic Games

Special sports programs for the mentally retarded are very popular. There are now *Special Olympic Games* for these players, which were first held in 1968 at Soldiers Field in Chicago. The game of basketball is one of the events on the program.

All-conference Teams

There are many different kinds of high-school and university conferences, or leagues. A conference is a group of teams that play against each other all through the season. Many high-school and university players are

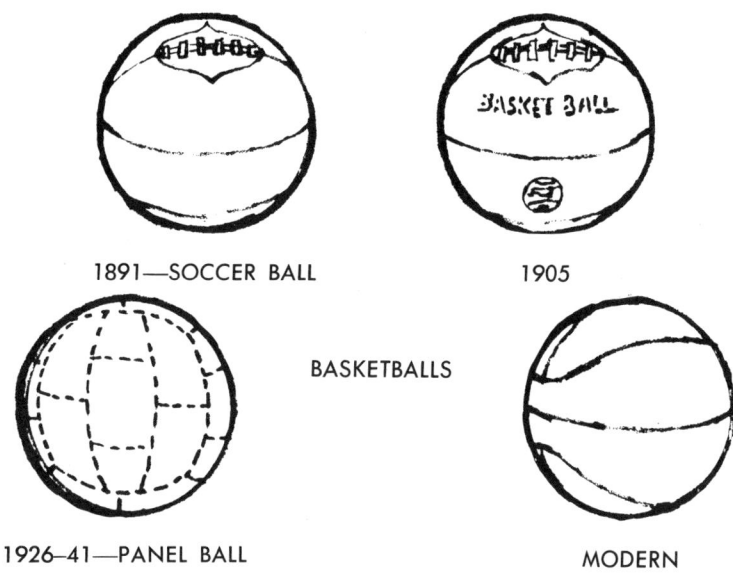

1891—SOCCER BALL   1905

BASKETBALLS

1926–41—PANEL BALL   MODERN

chosen as members of these all-conference teams.

National College Championship Games

One of the most popular contests is sponsored by the National Collegiate Athletic Association. The big universities and colleges belong to this league. At the end of every season these big schools play in tournaments to decide upon a National Championship team. The smaller colleges also have their national championship winner.

All-American

Every year the sportswriters and college coaches choose two All American Basketball

Teams, one for women and one for men. One player is chosen for each position. These players are the champions of their college or university teams from all over the United States.

The same committee also chooses a second team, and many other players receive honorable mention for their fine playing. These members had the best playing records for the season. Of course, it's a great honor to make these lists, especially to make the Basketball All-American!

Other Championship Games

1. There are Biddy Basketball Championship games for boys from 9 to 12 years of age and girls from 9 to 13 years. These players must be no more than 5 feet 6 inches tall. Biddy Basketball was started in 1950 by Jay Archer, a former physical-education director.
2. There are championships for Little Guys and Gals Basketball teams. These players are between 9 and 12 years of age and no more than 5 feet tall.
3. Youth Basketball Association leagues were developed in 1975 by the YMCA and the National Basketball Players' Association. Teams are organized for boys and girls in grades three to twelve. No league championships are recorded. Persons in charge

must see that every player gets a chance to play, have fun, and develop skills and sportsmanship.

World Olympic Games

Basketball is popular all over the world. Because so many people enjoy playing or watching this game, it was made a part of the World Olympic Games program in 1936. The first World Olympic competition for women's basketball began with the 1976 games in Montreal, Canada. Every four years many countries enter teams to decide the World Champions. The Olympic Basketball Tournaments are hard-fought games where many friendships are made.

Professional Basketball Teams

A professional team is made up of men who were top players on their college teams. These men get paid for playing. They play before great crowds in the large cities.

The best-known professional teams belong to the National Basketball Association. At the end of every season, the Association runs a tournament to decide the professional championship.

World-famous Globetrotters

The Globetrotters do not belong to the National Basketball Association. They are an independent professional team and make up their own playing schedule.

In addition to playing a smart game, they amuse the crowds by performing amazing tricks with basketballs. The Globetrotters are fast and fancy players. They are a popular team and play before great crowds in many parts of the world. This remarkable team has helped make the American game of basketball popular in many countries.

Chapter 2

Know Your Basketball

Basketball is exciting! It's fun to play this game, watch it, and read about it. Whether you are a player or a fan, you will enjoy basketball much more when you know the rules and understand the fine points.

Keep a basketball notebook. Write the rules in it. Put down other information that you learn. See how well you can predict the games. At the end of the season, look at your notebook and see how accurate you were in figuring the team and player records.

Know the Teams

Before going to a game, read the newspapers. The sports pages are filled with information about teams and players. Sportswriters often give the names of players, their schools, positions they play, and their numbers.

It is helpful to know the numbers of the players. Then at a game you can follow your favorite players on the court.

Idea of the Game

Two teams are on the court. Each team is assigned a basket. The idea of the game is to see which team can score the greatest number of points by getting the ball into its own basket the greatest number of times.

The team with the ball is on offense. Its players try to move the ball toward their own basket to make a score. You will notice that they move the ball by dribbling and passing.

The team without the ball is on defense. The players on this team use their guarding skills to keep the offensive team from scoring. They also try their best to get the ball away and over to their own basket so they can try for scores.

The Players

A basketball team is made up of five players. They are—two forwards, two guards, and one center.

Each player has regular duties. As soon as a team gets the ball, its two forwards and its center try to get close to their basket as quickly as possible. The two guards feed the ball to their center or forwards who are closer to the basket.

As the offensive team moves the ball near its basket, many plays are used so that every player, even the guards, may shoot for baskets and score.

As soon as the offensive team loses the ball, its players become the defensive team and their duties change. Now the two guards run to the other end of the court and try to prevent the enemy team from moving the ball closer to its basket. And the center and both forwards hurry into enemy territory and also start guarding to keep their opponents from making baskets. It's a "seesaw" battle as the ball travels back and forth from one end of the court to the other.

Length of Game

How long do teams play? It all depends upon the age group of the players.

High-school teams play four quarters of eight minutes each. There is a ten-minute rest period at the end of the first half-period of play. After the first and third quarters the players on boys' teams have one minute of rest and the girls have two minutes of rest.

College teams play two halves of twenty minutes each. They have fifteen minutes of rest between halves.

For younger players below high-school and junior high-school age, the game is divided into four quarters of six minutes each.

Playing Court

Did you know that basketball can be played on different-sized courts? *Court* is another name for a basketball playing area. The size of the court depends upon the age of the players.

High-school teams use a court 84 feet long and 50 feet wide. College teams play on a court 94 feet long and 50 feet wide. Both of these courts are divided in half by a line drawn through the center.

Younger players may use a court 60 feet long and 40 feet wide and that is divided into three parts.

All these courts have two backboards and baskets, one at each end of the playing area.

In the center of the court is a jump circle. There is a free throw line and free throw circle at each end of the court. Two lines connect each free throw circle to the end boundary lines. The area inside of these lines and the free throw circle is known as the *free throw lane.*

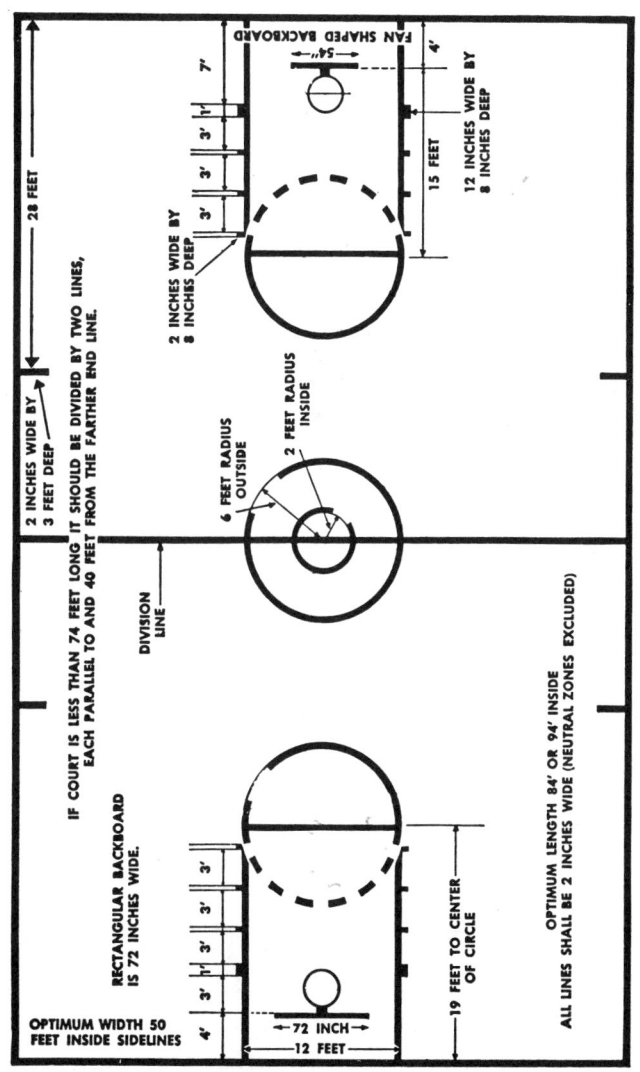

BASKETBALL COURT

Points in Scoring

A team can score points in two ways: through field goals and through free throws.
1. Field Goal
    When the ball goes into a basket during regular play, the team to which that basket belongs makes two points.
2. Free Throw
    This is a free shot given to a team that has been fouled. Each free throw that goes through the hoop is good for one point.

Fouls

There are two kinds of fouls that may occur in a game. They are *common* and *technical* fouls.

COMMON FOUL. A common, or personal, foul is made when a player holds, pushes, trips, or charges into an opponent. The player who was fouled is given one of three kinds of free throws, depending upon the seriousness of the foul.
1. In a foul where the damage to the player or team is very slight, the player may receive one free throw shot.
2. In a more serious foul, the referee may give the player who was fouled a "one-and-one," or "bonus" free throw. This means that the player has a chance to make *one* or

two points. If the first throw goes in, the player can take a second free throw. If that first free throw does not go into the basket, it becomes a free ball, and the player loses the chance to try for the second throw.
3. When a very serious foul occurs, the player who was fouled automatically receives two free throws. This means that even if the first free throw is missed, the player may still take the second free throw.

TECHNICAL FOUL. A technical foul is made:
1. When a player or team delays the game intentionally.
2. When a team takes too many time-outs.
3. When a player disobeys the game officials.
4. When a coach enters the playing court without the permission of the officials.

Whenever a technical foul takes place, the captain of the team against whom the foul was made chooses the best free thrower to try for the point. You can see how important it is to be a good free-throw shot.

In college or high-school games, a player is removed when five fouls are committed. Younger players must leave the game after they have made six fouls.

Moving the Ball

Players can move the ball by dribbling and by using different ways of passing.

PASSING. A pass is made when a player tosses the ball to a teammate who catches it. The pass may be made by a bounce, by a toss through the air, or by rolling the ball on the ground. The ball may also be handed to a teammate.

The ball may be passed from one teammate to another until it is in a good position to be thrown into the basket. If the ball is caught by an opposing player, it is an *intercepted pass.*

DRIBBLING. A dribble is made when a player taps the ball so that it bounces one or more times on the floor. Dribbling is a way of controlling the ball or keeping possession of it.

A player may dribble the ball while walking, running, or standing in one spot. When the dribbling action stops, the player may not start another dribble. This would be called an *illegal dribble.*

Official Signals

When a team breaks a rule it may pay a penalty. At the instant a rule is broken, the official blows a whistle and takes the ball. The official quickly makes certain hand signs that tell:
1. What the penalty is for.
2. Against which team it is being called.
3. Against which player it is being called.
4. What the penalty will be.

Substitutes

Every team has substitutes. These players must remain on the players' bench while a game is going on.

When a coach tells a substitute to enter the game, this player reports to the officials' table. The scorer quickly records the name, number, and position of the player. But the player doesn't run out on the court immediately. The substitute waits outside the playing area until a play ends. Then the scorer blows a horn to let the referee know that a substitute is coming out.

Additional Rules

College and high-school teams are allowed only five time-outs during a regular game. Younger players may have six time-outs. If a team takes more time-outs than are allowed, it is charged with a technical foul.

Jumping for a Held Ball

If two opponents have hold of the ball at the same time, this is called a "held ball." The referee takes the ball to the nearest jump circle and the two players involved must jump for it.

Out of Bounds

Any ball that goes past the boundary lines is considered out of bounds. The team that touched the ball last loses possession of it.

The official then gives the ball to a player on the opposing team at the spot where the ball went outside the court. This player must throw the ball back into play within five seconds.

Traveling with the Ball

Running while holding the ball is never allowed. This is called "traveling with the ball." When this happens the official takes the ball and hands it to a player on the opposing side. This player puts the ball back into play from outside the boundary lines.

Chapter 3

Footwork in Basketball

From the starting whistle to the end of the game, basketball players keep on the move. It's exciting to watch them as they get into position for their plays.

On the Move

Players run at full speed. They charge down the court and dribble. They make quick, running stops. They jump and pivot. A player needs good footwork to keep up with the ball or to get free from an opponent. All these skills are used whether the player has the ball or not. Smart footwork helps a team win games.

As an All-American coach once said, "No matter how good a shot you are, you must be able to get free from your opponent in order to receive the ball from a teammate so that you can shoot for a basket."

All-purpose Stance

The all-purpose stance gets you in a ready position to move swiftly into any play that may take place. Here is what you do:
1. Stand with your feet about shoulder-width apart, one foot slightly in front of the other, with the toes pointed a bit outward.
2. Bend the knees a little, keeping the shoulders a trifle forward.
3. Hold the arms a bit forward and sideward, with the fingers spread.

This is sometimes called a "wrestler's stance." But don't wrestle during a game! From this stance you can move forward, sideward, backward, or begin a quick run or jump. Later you will learn other stances for different plays.

The Running Start

Do you want to get free from your opponent? Would you like to run forward, to the side, or to the rear? This is the way to do it.

ALL-PURPOSE STANCE

THE RUNNING FORWARD START

RUNNING TO GET FREE

1. When you are in the all-purpose stance and want to run forward, push off with your rear foot and start the first step with your front foot. Continue to run forward and keep going with short, choppy steps.

2. When you are in the all-purpose stance and want to run toward the side or rear, pivot on your rear foot and step off with your front foot pointed in the direction in which you want to run. Push off with the rear foot and keep running.

To Make a Quick Running Stop

Many times during a game you must make a quick running stop. You must know how to make a running stop to avoid bumping into a player, to dribble, to shoot for a basket, to get free to receive a pass, and you can use it in many more situations. To make the running stop:
1. Come to a stop on your right foot and keep it firmly on the ground.
2. With your left foot, step out well in front of the right foot.
3. Keep from falling forward and balance yourself.

You are now ready for the coming play. Players can also come to a stop on the left foot and step out with the right foot.

The Jump Stop

The jump stop is a spectacular play. It is often used when you must jump up to get the ball. This stop can be made from a run or a stand:

1. Jump up and catch that ball!
2. Control the ball and land with both feet on the floor at the same time.
3. Steady yourself so that you will not fall over or take extra steps.

To make the jump stop from a run:
1. Stop and jump up for the ball.
2. Land with one foot ahead of the other to avoid falling forward.
3. Then go into the next play.

RUNNING STOP TO CATCH PASS

RUNNING JUMP STOP TO CATCH PASS

Using the Pivot Step

A pivot is a way to make a turn. All players use the pivot step because it helps a person move in any direction without wasting time. A pivot step can be used when you have or do not have the ball. It is a clever way to fake plays and fool your opponents.

To make a pivot step when you have the ball:

1. Take the all-purpose stance.
2. Raise the heel of the pivot foot and pivot on the ball of that foot.
3. Turn your body as you make the pivot, letting the free foot follow the direction of the turn.

Protect the ball by holding it close to your body. Bend slightly from the waist. Keep the elbows bent and extended outward in order to protect the ball from enemy players.

In this pivot, you can turn completely around or just make a quarter- or half-turn. But remember, the pivot foot must always remain on the floor while you turn, and the free foot may be moved in any direction and as many times as you wish.

If a player jumps for the ball and lands with both feet evenly on the floor, either foot may be used as the pivot foot.

If you land with one foot ahead of the other, you will pivot on the rear foot.

PIVOT STEP

Keeping Feet in Good Condition

As you can see, much of the game depends upon the feet. So you should try to strengthen your legs and keep your feet in good condition. To do this, try these exercises:

1. Skipping rope
2. Running in place with high knee action
3. Walking on the toes
4. Jumping up and down in place
5. Taking short sprints and making quick stops

PRACTICE DRILLS. *Without a ball.*

1. Stand in front of a good-sized mirror and take the all-purpose stance. Take a good look at yourself. Are your feet placed properly on the floor? Are the knees and arms in the right position?
2. From the stance position, practice quick running starts—forward, toward the side, and to the rear.
3. Run several yards using short, chopping steps, and then come to a full stop.
4. Run a few yards, stop, and pivot.
5. Run a few yards, jump, and stop.

Try these drills with a basketball in your hands. Then do them with one or more teammates. These drills are the same as those the champions practice.

Chapter 4

How to Guard

It's a tight game! The Panthers' star shooter is all over the floor. He tosses long shots and short ones and the points pile up. Can the Wildcats stop this "Dead-Eye Dick?"

All the Wildcat players jump into action and begin to guard their opponents. Their best guard puts extra pressure on this Panther sharpshooter. He guards closely and blocks the shots. The Panthers' scoring spree stops and the Wildcats pull the game out of the fire. A nice job of guarding!

Importance of Guarding

There is a saying in basketball, "You cannot score if your opponents won't let you."

So, when your opponents get possession of the ball, your team is on defense. This means that every player on your team now has the duty of guarding a certain opponent or a definite area of the playing court and must try to keep the enemy team from making baskets.

Facts About Guarding

To do a good job of guarding, every player on defense must learn the habits of the opponents. Is the player you are guarding fast or slow? Is the player left-handed? Does the player try to fake plays? Is the player in the habit of taking a jump before shooting?

Your team must try to find the answers to these questions as quickly as possible during a game. With this information your team can do a better job of keeping the opponents from making passes, from dribbling closer for scoring plays, and most important of all, from making shots at the basket.

Guarding Duties

Guarding duties are not always the same. The way you guard depends upon:
1. The kind of offensive formation your opponents use.

2. The kind of defensive formation your team is going to use to stop them.

However, if your opponents are not doing well during a game, they may shift into a different formation to fool your team. This means that your team will have to shift quickly into some other defensive formation so that all your players can do a better job of guarding.

All players must do guarding duty when their team is on defense. But the two players on the team who are officially named "guards" have some additional duties. These duties are:

1. At the tip-off, or jump ball, when two players jump for the ball, which is tossed into the air by an official, the two guards must stand in enemy territory ready to stop the enemy players who may catch the ball.
2. Every time your team makes a basket, it is the duty of your guards to be the first to run back quickly into enemy territory and keep the opponents from getting into scoring position.
3. When your team is making a free throw, these two guards do not have to stand near the free-throw lane. They may stand farther back on the court and be ready to prevent the enemy from moving toward their goal on the next play.
4. When your team causes the ball to go out of bounds, these two guards are the first to run back near the enemy goal to protect that area.

5. Often these guards are assigned to guard the best shooters on the enemy team.

Keep this fact in mind: No matter what position you play on the team, whether it be center, forward, or guard, *when your team is on defense, everyone on the team must know how to guard.* So study and learn the skills of guarding.

Distance between Guard and Opponent

There is no set rule that tells a guard how far away to stand from the opponent being guarded. This depends upon the play that is being made and where the opponent is on the court.

The distance at which you stand when guarding also depends upon how well you can move about on the floor, how well you can use your hands when trying to steal the ball, and how well you can block or steal the ball.

These are good general rules to remember:
1. Keep at least within arm's distance of your opponent when the ball is in the scoring area.
2. Stand about 5 feet away when your opponent is near the middle of the court, or too far away to score.

In other words, when the enemy has the ball near scoring position, all players on your team will guard as closely as possible. When your opponents are not near their scoring position, you do not have to stay so close to them.

But, if your team is behind and it is near the

end of the game, the strategy changes. This situation calls for guarding closely and tightly. It becomes your job to try to steal the ball or to force your opponent into making a bad play.

Don't be overanxious in your guarding and get too close to your opponent. If you do, you may commit a foul, and fouls don't win games.

All-purpose Guarding Stance

BOXER'S STANCE. Every player should learn the *boxer's stance*. This is very much like the one a boxer uses in the ring.
1. Stand comfortably with the feet spread, one foot a bit ahead of the other, and bend forward just a little.
2. If your right foot is forward, raise your right arm about head high, keeping the fingers spread.
3. Hold your left arm at the side, with your hand between knee and hip. Both arms should be slightly bent.
4. Move both arms about your opponent and watch every move the player makes.

This stance can also be done with the left foot forward and the left arm raised higher. The raised guarding arm prevents your opponent from shooting at a basket, tossing a high pass, or receiving a high pass. The lower guarding arm is ready to block low passes or dribbles.

This guarding movement is used when your opponent has or does not have the ball. You

can do your guarding in front, in back, or at the side of your opponent.

BOXER'S SHUFFLE. The boxer's shuffle is used for moving about quickly in any direction. It is very much like a sliding step.

To move toward the left, begin with the right foot and take a short shuffle-step toward the left. Take a short shuffle-step toward the left with the left foot. Continue with this shuffle-step and move where your opponent moves.

To move toward the right, start with the left foot and shuffle toward the right.

To shuffle forward, take a short step forward with the rear foot, shuffle forward with the front foot, and keep moving with your opponent.

To shuffle backward, take a short step backward with the front foot, shuffle backward with the rear foot, and stay with your opponent.

By shuffling swiftly and keeping close, a good guard can force the opponent toward the side lines or farther away from the goal. This pressure can force your enemy to make a bad play.

Guarding Offensive Player with the Ball

Stand at your guarding distance between your opponents' basket and the player you are guarding. Get into your all-purpose guarding stance. Move the raised arm about your opponent's face and move the lower arm at the side to hinder the player from making the next play.

Use the same guarding movements when your opponent does not have the ball, but be ready to prevent the player from getting free to receive passes.

Guarding the Pivot Player

Every team has a powerful player known as the "pivot" player. This pivot player is most often the center. The player is usually one of the tallest and best shooters on the team. This person knows how to make many kinds of shots and how to start new plays.

Usually the pivot player stands near the free-throw circle ready to receive the ball and

GUARDING PIVOT PLAYER

make a basket. Because this person is such a fine offensive player, it takes a top defender to perform the guarding duties.

To guard the pivot player who has the left shoulder toward the basket, take this guarding position:
1. Take a straddle position a bit behind and toward the pivot player's left.
2. Raise your right hand and keep it near the back of this player's right shoulder.
3. Hold your left hand near the pivot player's left side about waist high.

When the pivot player's right shoulder is toward the basket, do your guarding on this player's right side.

If the pivot player's back is facing the basket, you may use either of these guarding positions, but guard just a little toward the back.

If your pivot player is facing the basket, take a guarding position in front of this player.

Guarding a Dribbler

When a dribbler is too far away to shoot, take the all-purpose guarding stance between the dribbler and the basket. If the dribbling starts toward your left, be sure to stay a step ahead of the dribbler. Try to tap the ball away with your left hand in front of the dribbler when the ball is at the height of the bounce.

Be ready with your right hand to block a

GUARDING A STEP AHEAD OF DRIBBLER

sudden dribble toward the right. Keep a step ahead of the dribbling as you guard and try to force the dribbler toward the boundary lines.

Guarding After a Shot at Basket

There are times when you cannot prevent a player from shooting at the basket. When this happens, you can move into what is known as the *boxing-out* position to prevent your opponent from getting the ball on the rebound.

BOXING-OUT. After a shot is made at the basket, the defensive players near the basket move into the boxing-out position.

GUARDING DRIBBLER FROM REAR

The player who is guarding the shooter should move into the boxing-out position in this way:
1. Take your guarding position between the shooter and the opponent's basket.
2. After the shot is made, turn quickly, face the basket, stand in front of your opponent, and be ready to catch the rebound.

Your teammates who are also near the basket will move into the same position in front of the players they are guarding.

As you turned, you "boxed-out," or blocked, the path of the player you were guarding. Now your opponent has to travel all the way around you to try to recover the ball. And you are in a better position to get that ball yourself.

BOXING-OUT AFTER SHOT AT BASKET

Guarding for a Lay-up Shot

It's pretty hard to block a *lay-up shot* without committing a foul. Of course, the best thing is to try to prevent your opponent from getting into position to make the shot. But if the dribbler is able to move ahead of you in the drive toward the basket for a lay-up shot:
1. Run alongside until the dribbling stops.
2. When the opponent leaps for the basket, you should jump at the same time.
3. Stretch high with the arm that is closest to the shooter. Place this hand on the ball before it leaves the shooter's hands and try to block the shot.
4. Make a soft landing and balance yourself.

Guarding Hints
1. Always stay between your opponent and the basket.

BLOCKING LAY-UP SHOT

2. Learn to move and stay with your opponent.
3. If you must switch and guard another player, yell the word "Switch!" loudly for your teammates to hear.
4. Always put pressure on the dribbler and try to force the movement toward the side lines.

GUARDING DRILLS. *For one player without a ball.*

STANCE DRILL:
1. Take the all-purpose guarding stance.
2. Check your position and make corrections if needed.

FOOTWORK DRILL:
1. Practice the boxer's shuffle toward the left, toward the right, forward, and backward.
2. Use the boxer's shuffle and imagine you are guarding a dribbler. Force dribbler toward the side lines.

ACTION DRILLS. *For two or more players with a ball.*
1. A player on offense starts with a dribble from the middle of the court. The dribbler may move anywhere between the center line and the basket.

    A guard on defense keeps close and guards the dribbler.
2. Try the same drill with two teams of an equal number. The players of one team will guard the other team and try to keep them from passing, dribbling, or shooting.
3. Pressure Plays.

    A player on offense stands at the side line and throws the ball to a teammate. The defensive players try to block or steal the ball away.

    A pivot player stands near the foul line. A teammate throws a pass to the pivot player. One player will guard the passer, and the other will guard the pivot player.

GUARDING AGAINST TEN POINTS

This is a game for two or more players on a team, using only one half of a court and one basket. There should be an equal number of players on each team.

One offensive player starts the game by throwing the ball to a teammate from a spot anywhere along the side lines.

After the ball is in play, the offensive team tries to shoot the ball into the basket for two points, while the other team tries to prevent this scoring.

Every time the ball goes into the basket, the other team takes possession of it and puts it back into play from the side lines. Each time the ball does not go into the basket, it becomes a free ball and play continues. This is very much like a regular game. The first team to score ten points wins the game. The team that loses the game needs more guarding practice!

When a game is over, the player who has guarded with skill may not always stand out as a high scorer. A guard may not make any spectacular shots for the basket, but this player's guarding skills will have succeeded in keeping the ball near the goal or away from the opponents. Everyone knows that the guard's fine strategy has helped the team play a good game.

Chapter 5

Dribbling in Basketball

Many times during a game a player dribbles the ball down the court for a clean shot through the basket. Every player should know how to dribble. It is a means of moving the ball, controlling it, and making fake plays.

The Dribble Play

When a player taps the ball with one hand so that it bounces on the floor, this play is called a *dribble*. It can be a one-bounce dribble or a number of bounces.

Kinds of Dribbles

There are several kinds of dribbles. They are the low, high, change-of-hands, and change-of-direction dribbles.

After you can do these well, you may learn to dribble the ball on the run, while pivoting, and while changing hands and direction on the run. But don't hurry with the dribble plays. Learn them one at a time.

When to Use the Dribble

The dribble is used:
1. To move closer for a quick shot at the basket.
2. To keep control of the ball until a teammate can get free to catch your pass or hand-off.
3. To move toward a certain spot on the floor in order to get into a special team formation.

If you are closely guarded anywhere on the court and cannot pass the ball, use the dribble to make a getaway.

The Low Dribble

The low dribble is used when a player is surrounded by opponents. It is a good way of protecting and controlling the ball until you can pass it.

STATIONARY LOW DRIBBLE

Stance for Low Dribble
1. Bend the knees to an almost half-crouch position.
2. Spread the fingers of the dribble hand and form a cup.
3. Keep your head up.
4. Hold your free hand at your side ready to use for protection and balance.

You are now ready to dribble the ball.

Making the Low Dribble

To make the *low dribble from a standing-still position*, push the dribble hand downward and tap the ball lightly with the fingers, using an easy flick of the wrist. Regulate the tap so that the ball will bounce about knee-high. Bend the

LOW DRIBBLE ON THE RUN

elbow of the dribble arm after every tap of the ball to get ready for another tap.

To make the *low dribble on the run,* place the dribble hand a trifle behind the ball and push it downward and forward. Make these dribbles by tapping the ball so that it bounces about 12 to 15 inches ahead of you. Continue to flick the ball using this forward-downward motion with every step you take.

Remember: The faster you run, the farther forward you must bounce the ball.

Be careful to protect the ball. Watch out for enemy players who may be close by!

As you practice, keep these facts in mind:

1. A basketball has plenty of bounce. It doesn't take much of a push to make it rebound from the floor.
2. Do not *bat* the ball with your hand. It may bounce too high and your opponent will steal it.

The High Dribble

When enemy players are not close and the court is open, you can charge away with speed by using the high dribble.

Stance for High Dribble

1. Lean a trifle forward.
2. Bend the knees as you would for a comfortable running position.
3. Cup the dribble hand with the fingers well spread.
4. Hold your free arm at your side for protection and balance. Look straight ahead.
   You are ready to dribble the ball.

Making the High Dribble

From a standing-still position, tap the ball hard enough so it will bounce about waist-high.

HIGH DRIBBLE ON THE RUN

After every tap be ready with the dribble hand to start the next bounce.

To make the *high dribble on the run,* bend forward just a little. Then push the ball forward hard enough so that it will bounce about waist-high and will not slow down your run.

Remember this fact: The farther you push the ball in front, the faster you must run to keep up with it.

Change-of-hands Dribble

When you are surrounded by enemy players, you may wish to change hands to protect the ball.

Stance for Change-of-hands Dribble

1. If you have an open court with a clear field ahead, take the high-dribble stance.
2. If you are in a crowded area, take the low-dribble stance.

Making the Change-of-hands Dribble

Start the dribble with your right hand. To change hands on the dribble, give the ball an easy tap, pushing it with the right hand so that it will cross in front of your body and land near your left toe. Continue the dribble with your left hand.

CHANGE-OF-HANDS DRIBBLE

You may change back and use your best dribble hand as soon as you are free for the next play. This dribble can be started with either hand and can be done while you are standing still or on the run.

The change-of-hands dribble can also be used to fake a player out of position or to get into a better spot on the court.

Fake Shot and Dribble

There are many ways to get free from an opponent and start a dribble. One way is to go through the motions of making a two-handed shot into the basket.

As the hand of your opponent is raised to block this fake shot, bring the ball down in front of you and bend your knees. Make a quick turn toward the right by crossing the left foot over toward the right side.

Keep your body low, start your dribble with

FAKE SHOT AND DRIBBLE

the right hand (which is farthest from your opponent), and charge past the left side of the player guarding you. To charge past your opponent's right side after the fake shot, start the dribble with your left hand.

Faking Change-of-direction Dribble

To fake a dribble toward the left, go through all the motions of making the dribble. Move the ball, your head, and left foot to make the dribble look real.

As your guarding opponent moves toward your left, cross over with your left foot toward the right, and start a low dribble with your right hand. This faking play can be done toward the right using the opposite hand and foot.

CHANGE-OF-HANDS DRIBBLE

You may change back and use your best dribble hand as soon as you are free for the next play. This dribble can be started with either hand and can be done while you are standing still or on the run.

The change-of-hands dribble can also be used to fake a player out of position or to get into a better spot on the court.

Fake Shot and Dribble

There are many ways to get free from an opponent and start a dribble. One way is to go through the motions of making a two-handed shot into the basket.

As the hand of your opponent is raised to block this fake shot, bring the ball down in front of you and bend your knees. Make a quick turn toward the right by crossing the left foot over toward the right side.

Keep your body low, start your dribble with

FAKE SHOT AND DRIBBLE

the right hand (which is farthest from your opponent), and charge past the left side of the player guarding you. To charge past your opponent's right side after the fake shot, start the dribble with your left hand.

Faking Change-of-direction Dribble

To fake a dribble toward the left, go through all the motions of making the dribble. Move the ball, your head, and left foot to make the dribble look real.

As your guarding opponent moves toward your left, cross over with your left foot toward the right, and start a low dribble with your right hand. This faking play can be done toward the right using the opposite hand and foot.

FAKE CHANGE-OF-DIRECTION DRIBBLE

Double Dribble

There are two kinds of double dribbles, the *legal* and *illegal*. A double dribble is legal when you dribble the ball, catch and hold it in your hands, and an opponent touches it but does not get it away.

Rule: When an opponent touches the ball after a player has stopped dribbling, this player may begin another series of dribbles.

A double dribble is illegal when you stop the dribble, hold the ball, and start another series of dribbles.

Rule: When a player stops dribbling, holds the ball, then starts dribbling again, this second series of dribbles is illegal, and the ball goes to the other team.

Dribbling Hints

Opposing players are always on the alert to steal or tap the ball out of a dribbler's hands. Many players lose the ball while dribbling because they don't protect it. To have good ball protection:

1. Always dribble with the hand farthest away from your opponent. Make sure that your free hand is between you and your opposing player and use it for protection.
2. When you are using the low dribble and your opponents are behind you, protect the ball with your body by crouching low and dribbling the ball in front of you.
3. If you are dribbling with the right hand and an opponent comes toward you on the right, change the dribble to the left hand or turn your back toward the opponent and continue to dribble.
4. Do not dribble blindly. Always be on the alert to pass the ball to a teammate.
5. Don't get into the habit of taking a one-bounce dribble every time you get possession of the ball. This play may force you to pass or shoot for a basket no matter where you may be standing on the court.

PRACTICE DRILLS

Begin your drills from a standing-still position and work slowly toward the faster-action dribbling plays.

STANCE DRILL. *For one player without a ball.*
Take the low-dribble stance and check yourself. Are your knees in a half-crouch position? Is your free hand at the side? Take this position over and over again, until it becomes easy to do.

STANCE AND DRIBBLE DRILL. *For one player with a ball.*
1. With the ball in your hands, take the stance for the:
    a. Low dribble
    b. High dribble
    c. Change-of-hands dribble.
2. Then take each stance one at a time and go into the dribble.

FAKE SHOT AND DRIBBLE DRILL. *For one player.*
1. Without a ball, go through all the motions of the fake shot and dribble:
    a. Toward the left
    b. Toward the right.
2. Do the same drills using a ball.
3. Practice these drills with a player guarding you.

FAKE AND CHANGE-OF-DIRECTION DRIBBLE
1. Practice the fake and change-of-direction dribble alone and with a ball.
2. Try this drill with an opponent guarding you.

PROTECTING-THE-BALL EXERCISE. *For two players.*
1. Start a dribble with a walk or slow run.
2. Have a second player run behind you and try to steal the ball away.
3. See how well you can protect the ball while dribbling.
4. Change places and let your partner dribble the ball while you try to steal it.

When you can do these drills well you are on the road to becoming a good player.

DRIBBLE RELAY GAME

This game can be played by two or more teams with an equal number of players on each team.
1. Each team of players forms two rows. The two rows face each other at a distance of 10 yards apart.
2. The first player in one row dribbles toward his teammate who is at the head of the line on the opposite side.
3. This player takes the ball and dribbles back to the next teammate on the other side.

    At the end of the dribble every player takes his place at the end of the line.

    The team whose starting player is first to reach his own place wins the game.

    Try to make up some dribble relay games of your own.

Chapter 6

Shooting for Baskets

It is important to know how to handle a basketball and how to dribble and pass. These skills are needed to get the ball in place to set up the shots. But shooting for baskets is really the "backbone" of the game. It's the points that count, and the team that makes the baskets wins the games.

The Different Shots

A champion player knows how to make many kinds of shots and when to use each one. The shots used most often in a game are:

1. The two-hand set shot
2. The free-throw shot
3. The one-hand set shot
4. The lay-up shot
5. The one-hand jump shot
6. The hook shot.

These shots can be made from a run, jump, pivot, or stationary position. You can make long or short shots from the side, in front, or underneath the basket. When you can learn to make that ball whip through the hoop without missing, you will become a "Dead-eye Dick."

Set Shots

When a player stops and gets "set" before aiming for the basket, the play is called a set shot. Every set shot is made with both of the player's feet on the floor. These shots are often known as "push" shots.

Stance and Grip for Two-hand Set Shot

The two-hand set shot can be made from a position farther out on the court than can any other shot. To make this shot:
1. Stand with your feet close together and even. (Or, you may place one foot slightly ahead of the other.)
2. Bend the knees a bit and keep your weight evenly divided on both feet.
3. Grip the ball with both hands and hold it a few inches away from your chin. Keep the

fingers well spread upon the ball with the thumbs toward the back, acting as a guide.
4. Keep the body straight from the waist up.
5. Look at the near side of the basket rim.

Making the Two-hand Set Shot

1. Bend the knees.
2. At the same time bend the wrists back so that the ball rests upon the hands. The fingers of both hands should point upward.
3. Straighten the knees as you move the arms forward and upward. Push the ball toward the basket and let it leave your fingertips at eye level with a quick snap of the wrists.

Follow-through for Two-hand Set Shot

Follow through with the arms stretched toward the flight of the ball with the palms facing slightly outward. Recover your balance and get ready for the next play.

To make a longer shot, place your hands closer together behind the ball, push harder with the knees, and make the throw with more force. For shorter shots, take the regular grip, and do not push the ball so hard.

Making the Free Throw

The free throw is always made from a set standing position. It can be made in several

GRIP FOR TWO-HAND SET SHOT

TWO-HAND SET SHOT

ways, the *two-hand underhand shot, one-hand push shot*, and *two-hand overhead push shot*. To make the two-hand underhand shot:
1. Stand with the toes just behind the free-throw line and feet shoulder-width apart.

2. Grip the ball with both hands, arms stretched about waist-high, and keep your fingers spread just a little under the center of the ball.
3. Bend the knees to an almost half-crouch position and at the same time move the ball downward until it reaches midpoint between the knees. Your fingers are now pointed downward.

TWO-HAND UNDERHAND FREE THROW

4. Straighten the knees and bring the ball forward and upward while keeping your eyes on the near side of the rim.
5. Stretch the arms fully and, when the ball reaches about chin or head level, make the throw with an upward wrist snap. The ball should be released from the fingertips.

Follow through with the toes on the floor, legs straight, and arms stretched toward the basket. Now get set for a rebound ball or the next play.

Practice the two-hand underhand shot until you can get the ball right into the basket. As you grow bigger and improve on your accuracy skills, you may try the other kinds of free throws.

Overhead Free Throw Push Shots

The one-hand and two-hand free throw push shots are made in almost the same way as the one-hand and two-hand set shots. The only difference is that in the free throw, no opponents will be allowed to rush your "free" shots to the basket.

Stance and Grip for One-hand Set Shot

This shot is handy when you are close to the basket because it can be made more quickly than the two-hand set.

After dribbling the ball or receiving a pass,

make the set shot with the right hand in this way:
1. Come to a complete stop.
2. Bend the knees just a bit, and stand with the right foot a little ahead of the other.
3. Grip the ball by cupping the left hand under it with well-spread fingers. The fingers of the left hand should point straight ahead. Place the right hand behind and just above the center of the ball. The well-spread fingers of the right hand are pointed upward. (The ball should not touch or rest upon the palm of the hand.)
4. Raise the ball about chin-high. Look directly over the top of the ball toward the near side of the rim.

Making the One-hand Set Shot

1. With the weight on the right (front) foot, start to shift the ball into the right hand by bending the right wrist backward so that the ball rests upon the right hand. The left hand acts as a guide.
2. Straighten the legs and begin to raise the right arm, keeping the left hand on the ball.
3. Whip the right hand upward and forward toward the goal with a smooth wrist action and remove the left hand just before the ball leaves the fingertips.

To get more distance on the throw, push off harder on the front foot and take a short shuffle-step forward at the end of the throw.

GRIP FOR ONE-HAND SET SHOT

ONE-HAND SET SHOT

Follow-through for One-hand Set Shot

After the shot, keep the left (free) hand about chin-high. The shooting hand and fingers are now pointed in the direction of the throw.

With your eyes still on the target, take a position with your weight equally divided on both feet. You are now ready to move in any direction for the next play. This shot can also be made with the left hand.

Making the Lay-up Shot

Lay-ups can be made from the right or left side, or from a position directly in front of the basket. To make the lay-up shot from the right side of the basket:

1. With your eyes on the target, dribble toward the basket, keeping the ball close to the floor.
2. When you reach within one or two steps of

LAY-UP SHOT

the basket, lift the ball with both hands, keeping the left hand on the bottom and the right (shooting) hand behind the ball.
3. At the same time raise the right knee as high as possible and jump off the floor with the left foot.
4. At the highest point of the jump, shift the ball from the left into the right hand.
5. Raise the right arm high overhead and push the ball carefully against the backboard or just over the rim.

On the follow-through come down on the floor with both feet and get into position for the next play.

To make this shot from the left side, shoot

ONE-HAND JUMP SHOT

with your left hand, raise the left foot, and jump off with the right foot.

When shooting from directly in front of the basket, use either the right or left hand but be sure to raise off the floor the foot that is on the same side as the shooting hand.

Making the One-hand Jump Shot

This is a very popular shot because it can be done so quickly. The one-hand jump shot can be started from a stationary position, after you receive a pass, or after a series of dribbles.

4
5

To make the one-hand jump shot with the right hand, after you have dribbled the ball:
1. Come to a complete stop with the right foot a trifle forward. Place your weight on it.
2. Hold the ball about chest-high with the left hand underneath and the right (shooting) hand behind it.
3. Bend the knees and get into position to make a jump.
4. Jump up with a good knee kick, and as you reach the peak of the jump, make a little "down-and-up" motion with both hands.
5. Bend the right wrist back so the ball rests upon the right hand. Complete the forward and upward motion, and with a flick of the wrist push the ball toward the basket. Keep the left hand on the ball until the last moment before it leaves your right hand.

Follow through with the fingers pointing toward the direction of the throw. Land on both feet with the knees bent a little.

For left-handers, come to a stop with the left foot a bit forward. Hold the ball upon the right hand and place the left hand behind it.

Making the Hook Shot

The hook shot is also known as the *pivot shot*. It is made with your back turned toward the basket. After dribbling the ball or catching a pass with a guard in front of you, get into position by turning your back to the basket.

RIGHT-HAND HOOK SHOT

Then:
1. Come to a complete stop with the left foot a little ahead of the right.
2. Raise the right knee, make a quarter-turn toward the left, and look at the target. Your left shoulder is now facing the basket, and you are holding the ball in both hands chest-high and away from the body.
3. Shift the ball to the right hand, stretch the right arm, and with a high-curved sweep, shoot over your head and into the basket.
4. At the end of the throw, complete the turn so that your whole body is facing the basket.
5. Make a soft landing on both feet with the knees bent and get ready for a rebound or the next play.

Follow through with the fingers of the right

(shooting) hand pointing toward the left shoulder.

This shot can also be made with the left hand. Always make the hook shot with the hand farthest away from the basket. This makes it hard for opponents to block the shot.

Additional Shots at the Basket

Learn to do the basic shots first for they are the ones you will use most often. When you can do them smoothly, treat yourself to some extra fun and try these challenging plays:

TIP-IN SHOT. Tip-in shots are usually made after a ball rebounds from the backboard or rim. To make a tip-in shot:
1. Leap high for the rebound ball.
2. Let it land in your hand for less than a split second.
3. Quickly straighten the arm and jump.
4. At the high point of the jump, tap the ball, with fingers spread, toward the basket again.

When this play is made with speed, it looks as though the ball barely touched the fingertips.

CROSSING-UNDER-BASKET SHOT. If you want to make a shot from the left side of the basket and you see you have dribbled too far to make it:

1. Continue the dribble until you are under the basket.
2. Quickly shift the ball to your right hand.
3. Raise the right knee, jump up with the left foot, and make a hook shot from the right side of the basket.

This shot can also be made from the left side of the basket with the left hand making the throw.

Two-hand Jump Shot. This is very much like the one-hand jump shot except that the ball is held evenly with both hands. The fingers are spread upon the ball with the thumbs almost touching behind it. To make the two-hand jump shot:
1. Come to a quick stop.
2. Make a high jump.
3. At the height of the jump make a down-and-up motion with both hands and flip the ball toward the basket.
4. Make a soft landing with the knees slightly bent.

Jump-turn Shot. If you are closely guarded from the rear and your back is toward the basket:
1. Leap up with a good knee action.
2. While your body is off the ground, make a half-turn and face the basket.
3. Stretch the arms and with a forward motion of the wrists flip the ball into the basket.

This shot can be made with the right or left hand, and also with both hands. To make the shot with the right hand, turn left on the jump. For a left-hand shot, make a right turn on the jump. You may also use both hands to make this shot.

SHOOTING DRILLS

All through these drills be sure to grip the ball correctly. You will soon find out which shots are more natural for you to do. But learn the other shots in case you need them.

STANCE AND GRIP DRILL
1. Practice all the stances for the different shots.
2. Work on the proper grip for the shots.
3. Take the stance and grip for each of the shots.

SOLO SHOOTING DRILL

Practice the different shots whenever you can. This may be in your own backyard (if you have a basket), on the playground, or in a gymnasium.

SOLO SHOOTING GAMES
1. Choose a certain shot and try it from different positions on the floor.
2. Decide upon a certain number of tries for the basket—perhaps ten. Keep score and see how many shots out of the ten go through the hoop. Now see how many out of twenty shots hit the target.

3. Play this game with one or more friends. They will recover the ball after every throw and send it back to you. Every player should have a turn shooting baskets. The one with the highest score wins the game.

FREE-THROW GAME. *For two or more players.*

Decide upon a certain number of free-throw shots. Keep a record and see which player can make the most free throws within that number. The player with the highest score wins the game.

LONG- AND SHORT-SHOT GAME, OR "21." *For two or more players.*

A player stands anywhere on the court behind the free-throw line and takes a long shot at the basket. The player then goes after the ball, gets it on the rebound, dribbles, and takes a short shot at the basket. Or, the player may take a short shot without dribbling.

Two points are scored for every long shot and one point for each short one that goes through the basket. The first player to score twenty-one points wins the game.

This game shows a player which shots s/he can do well and which need more practice.

ADVANCED DRILLS

This may be called a *pressure practice drill* because the plays are set up as they would be during a real game.

In this advanced drill try the different shots from any place on the court. An opposing player guards you and tries to keep the ball from going into the basket.

As you improve in shooting, the guards will put on more pressure and guard more closely. You will find that as the pressure grows greater this game becomes more exciting.

Practice this drill until you are able to outwit the guards and really get that ball through the hoop. Every player should have a chance to be a shooter and a guard.

Before long you will get that ball to whip through the basket. And those baskets run up the score for winning games.

Chapter 7

Passing in Basketball

Every player on the team should know how to throw a basketball to a teammate. This is known as "passing" the ball. Passing is a means of moving the ball toward the basket. It is also a way of sending the ball to a teammate when you are trapped or closely guarded. A good passer must know how and when to use each pass.

The Different Passes

Older players use many kinds of passes. At present, you do not need to know all of them.

Learn the passes you will use most often. Mix these passes with dribbling, running, and change-of-pace plays and you will have a fast-moving game like the older players. The passes are:
1. Two-hand chest pass
2. Two-hand underhand pass
3. Two-hand bounce pass
4. Two-hand overhead pass
5. Hook pass
6. Hand-off pass
7. Fake pass.

Two-hand Chest Pass

The two-hand chest pass is the most widely used. It is also known as the "chest push-pass." This pass is used for making short, quick, accurate throws.

TWO-HAND CHEST PASS

1   2

Grip for Two-hand Chest Pass

1. Grip the ball with both hands chest high and a few inches away from the body.
2. Spread the fingers along both sides of the ball. The fingers should point forward and the thumbs should be behind the ball. The pressure on the ball should come from the fingers while the thumbs act as a guide for the throw. The palms of the hands do not touch the ball.

Stance for Two-hand Chest Pass

1. Lean slightly forward from the waist.
2. Bend the knees just a bit.
3. Place one foot a little ahead of the other.

You are now in position to look for your receiver and are ready to throw the pass.

Making the Two-hand Chest Pass

1. Bring the elbows back quickly and bend the wrists so that the fingers point upward. The ball is now close to your chest.
2. Take a short, fast step with the forward foot.
3. At the same time, push as far as your arms will go and snap the ball with a good wrist action toward your receiver. As the ball leaves your hands the palms will face downward.

Follow-through for Two-hand Chest Pass

Follow through by stretching the arms forward as far as possible. Then recover your balance by taking a short hop or step forward as you straighten your body.

A good follow-through gives the ball a "reverse spin" just as it leaves the fingers. This spin helps the ball travel faster and makes it easier to catch.

Grip and Stance for Two-hand Underhand Pass

This is a good pass to use when a player is guarding in front of you with his arms up high and close to you, or at any other time when it is safe to use this pass. Use the same grip as for the two-hand chest pass but hold the ball waist-high and close to your body.

Stand with the left foot a little ahead of the

TWO-HAND UNDERHAND PASS

right. Lean forward from the waist and bend the knees so that you are in an almost half-crouch position.

Making the Two-hand Underhand Pass

1. Take a quick step forward with the left foot.
2. Move the ball to your right side at waist

level with the fingers spread and pointing downward. The elbows are bent a bit and held away from the body.
3. Stretch your arms forward and snap the wrists as you pass the ball under the arms of the player who is guarding you. As the ball leaves your fingertips, your palms will face each other.

Follow-through for Two-hand Underhand Pass

Stretch your arms forward in the direction of your receiver. At the end of the forward-downward motion, take a short step or hop on the left (front) foot and let the rear foot come forward. This pass may be made from either side of the body. If the right foot is forward, the toss is made from the left side.

Stance and Grip for Two-hand Bounce Pass

Here is another pass you may use when you find yourself guarded closely in front by a player's hands held waist high or above. Use the same grip as for the two-hand chest pass, but hold the ball about waist high. Bend the knees rather deeply with one foot ahead of the other. Lean forward and protect the ball.

Watch your opponent. Look to see where your target (receiver) is going to be, but try to keep your opponent from knowing where you intend to pass.

TWO-HAND BOUNCE PASS

Making the Two-hand Bounce Pass

Spot the position of your receiver. Then bend your knees deeper so that the rear knee will be quite close to the floor. Straighten the arms and toss the ball in a downward and forward direction with a nice flip of the wrists. As the ball leaves your hands, the fingers and palms should face downward. The ball will bounce in front of your receiver about waist-high.

After the throw, follow through by keeping the arms stretched forward and downward. Take a quick step forward to recover your balance.

Stance and Grip for Two-hand Overhead Pass

The overhead pass is used when you have to throw the ball over the arms of an opponent who is guarding you, or when you make a high toss to a teammate.

Take the same grip as for the two-hand chest pass, but place your spread fingers a little more behind the ball.

Stand with your feet about shoulder-width apart and with the knees bent a little. Raise your arms so that your hands are just above your head and a bit forward. Your fingers are now pointed upward.

Making the Two-hand Overhead Pass

Take a quick, short step forward with the knees bent a little. At the same time bend the wrists backward so that the ball is lying in your cupped hands.

Stretch the arms forward and upward and push with the wrists. With this push the ball leaves your hands. As the ball leaves the

TWO-HAND OVERHEAD PASS

1

2

fingertips, the palms of your hands should face downward.

Follow through by shifting your weight to the front foot. Finish the throw with your arms stretched out toward your receiver. Very often this pass is made with a jump.

Advanced Passes

Are you beginning to "whip" these passes across the court? Can you get that ball away from the tall players and hardworking guards? Then you are ready to try these next passes.

HOOK PASS. This is quite a fancy pass. When a guard is standing close behind you and there is no teammate in front to whom you can pass the ball, here is what you can do:

1. Protect the ball by holding it close to your body, about waist-high.
2. Keep your weight on the left foot.
3. With both hands bring the ball up about shoulder-high.
4. Pivot on the left foot and turn your body around toward your receiver.
5. Start shifting the ball by taking the left hand away and letting the ball rest on the whole of your right hand.
6. Quickly whip this passing arm upward with a half-circle motion toward your receiver.

Follow through with the knees bent to get your balance. This pass can be done with the

HOOK PASS

HAND-OFF PASS

right or left hand. It can also be made with a short jump on the pivot foot.

HAND-OFF PASS. This pass is used when a player wishes to fool the person who is guarding. It is also a good pass for getting out of a tight situation.

If you are being guarded closely from behind and there is no one to whom you can throw the ball, here is what you do:
1. Lean forward and protect the ball by keeping it close to your body about waist-high.

2. At this moment a teammate runs in front of you. Quickly hand the ball to the player as s/he passes by. Fine timing, excellent teamwork, and you're out of a spot!

Faking a Pass

To fake a pass you should look in one direction while you pass the ball in another. Or, you may pretend to throw the ball up high but instead throw a low pass. If necessary make some other faking movements.

Helpful Passing Hints
1. If your hands are small and you wish to make the two-hand chest shot, place your hands more behind the ball with the fingers spread and the thumbs quite close together.
2. In the two-hand bounce pass, try to make the ball land in front of your receiver at about waist height.
3. Be alert to hear a call for a pass from a teammate.
4. If your receiver is on the move, aim the pass so that the ball will reach in front of that player.
5. Know when it is best to use a high half-circle curve, low curve, or straight line pass.

PASSING DRILLS

STANCE AND GRIP DRILL. *For one player.*
1. Practice the stances for the different passes without a ball.

2. Practice the stance and grip for the different passes with a ball.

Shifting the Ball

Hold the ball with both hands. Make sure the fingers and thumbs are well spread. Shift the ball from one hand to the other. Practice this exercise until you can do it easily without dropping the ball.

Target Practice

1. Mark a target on a wall, garage, or barn. Make sure to choose a strong place so that there will be no damage to any property.
2. Practice the simple passes in slow motion against the target. When you learn to hit the target, try the more advanced passes.

These exercises, which you practice alone, give you the opportunity of working at a certain skill until you have mastered it. Then when you begin the partner drills, you can concentrate on timing and speed.

partner drills

1. With a partner, practice the different passes from a standing-still position. One player acts as the passer, and the other is the receiver.
2. Try these passes while the receiver is on the run.

Target Partner Drill

1. Mark a target on a wall. One player is the

passer, and the other will act as an opposing guard.
2. The passer will try to send the ball to the wall target. Your opponent will guard closely and try to prevent you from tossing the pass.

Three-player Drill

One player is the passer, one is a guard, and the other is the receiver.

The passer will toss short, easy throws to a receiver who is standing still. The guard tries to prevent the passer from sending the ball to the receiver.

After you can do this drill smoothly, try the passes at a moving target. This means that you will throw the ball to a receiver who is running.

Everyone should have a chance to play each position. These drills will help you learn to play a smooth passing game. It takes fine teamwork to make smart plays.

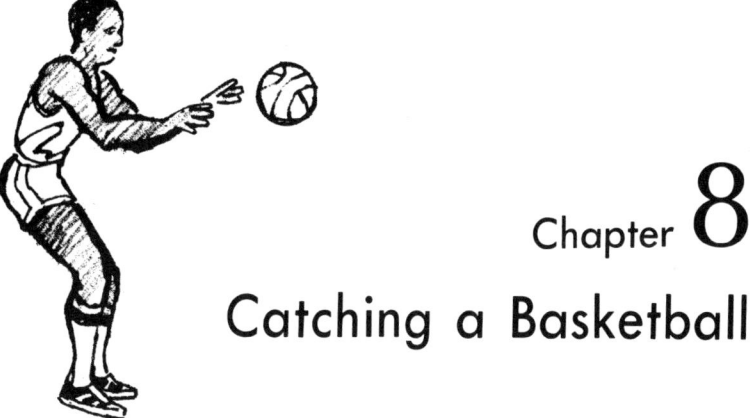

Chapter 8
Catching a Basketball

The game is almost over with only fifteen seconds left to play. The score is: Tigers—40, Lions—41.

Tiger Tina has the ball but is quite a distance from her basket, and she is being closely guarded by a Lion player. Tina pivots and makes a swift pass to her teammate, Eileen, who is closer to the basket. Eileen leaps high into the air and makes a two-handed catch. With great speed she dribbles and sinks the ball right into the basket. The Tigers win by one point. A beautiful play!

Catching Helps Win Games

The difference between winning and losing a game may depend upon whether or not a player knows how to catch a ball. If a player fails to make a catch and the other team gets possession of the ball, the game may be lost. The team with the ball is the team that has the chance to score.

Every player should know how to make the different catches. They are:
1. Stationary catch (above the waist, below the waist, above the head)
2. Jump catch
3. Running catch
4. On-the-bounce catch
5. Rolling-ball catch.

After making a catch, hold onto the ball. Then take the proper position to dribble, to pass, or to shoot for a basket.

Stationary Catch

A stationary catch is made while the player is standing still. However, before making any catch it is necessary for the player to take the correct stance.

ALL-PURPOSE STANCE OR ABOVE-THE-WAIST STANCE. In basketball there is a position that may be called the *all-purpose stance.* It is a natural stance position. A player usually takes this stance all through a game, because this stance allows the player to shift into any position necessary to catch the ball. This is known as the *above-the-waist* stance.

To make a stationary catch when the ball is coming toward you above the waist, take this stance:

1. Stand with your feet spread about shoulder-width apart. One foot is a little ahead of the other and pointed toward the path of the ball.
2. Bend the knees slightly and lean forward a bit from the hips.
3. Stretch the arms forward with the elbows slightly bent.
4. Keep your eyes on the ball. You are now ready to make the catch.

Above-the-waist Catch

1. Face the ball.
2. Form a cup to catch the ball by spreading the fingers of both hands with the palms facing the ball, fingers pointing upward and the thumbs almost touching.
3. Catch the ball with a firm grip. Use all the fingers and the upper part of the palms when you make the catch.
4. At the moment the ball reaches your hands, bring it toward your body with the movement of the catch. This will prevent the ball from popping out of your hands.
5. Protect the ball from your opponent. You are now ready to make the next play.

ALL-PURPOSE STANCE

ABOVE-THE-WAIST CATCH

BELOW-THE-WAIST CATCH

Below-the-waist Stance

A ball is coming toward you below the waist. You are standing in the all-purpose above-the-waist stance. To catch this low ball you will have to shift into a different position.

Bend the knees deeper so that you are in a half-crouch position. Stretch the arms forward and a bit downward. Bend the elbows a little. You are now in position to catch that ball.

Below-the-waist Catch

Form a cup to catch the ball. The palms of both hands face the ball. Spread the fingers so that the little fingers of both hands are almost touching and pointed downward. Make the catch and get ready for the next play.

Above-the-head Catch

A ball is coming toward you above your head. You are standing in the natural above-the-waist stance.
1. Stretch both arms upward with palms of hands facing the ball.
2. Form a cup to receive the ball.
3. As the ball touches the fingers, control it by bringing it down close to your waist.
4. Get ready to dribble, pass, or shoot.

Jump Catch

The jump catch is higher than the above-the-head catch. This play is made in the air with your feet off the ground. To make the jump catch:

JUMP CATCH

RUNNING CATCH AND DRIBBLE

1. Bend the knees just a little.
2. Jump up from the balls of your feet. While you are in the air, catch the ball.
3. Control the ball and land with bent knees on the balls of the feet.

Warning! Do not take extra steps after landing on the floor with the ball.

Running Catch

No matter what the direction of your run may be, always be ready to shift into the pass-catching position that will be best for you. As you run, form a target with well-spread fingers, hands cupped above or below the waist, depending upon the height of the ball as it reaches you.

Catch the ball while on the run. Be sure to make a running stop as soon as the ball reaches your hands. After you make the catch, you may wish to start a quick dribble or pass without stopping the run.

On-the-bounce Catch

Many passes are thrown on the bounce. As the ball is thrown, try to judge it quickly and get into position to catch it as it is coming toward you. To catch these passes, use the stance that is best for the bounces thrown, whether they come fast or slow, high or low.
1. If the bounce is above the waist, use the above-the-waist stance.
2. If the bounce is below the waist, use the below-the-waist stance.
3. If the bounce is above the head, use the above-the-head stance.
4. If the bounce is to the right or left of you, use the stance that is best, but be sure to stretch your arms toward the path of the ball.

Rolling-ball Catch

To catch a rolling ball, bend the knees so that they almost touch the floor.

Form a cup to receive the ball. Your hands are close to the floor with fingers outstretched and pointed downward. Stop or "trap" the ball and pick it up from the floor. Protect it from your opponents and get set to dribble, pass, or shoot for a score.

Helpful Hints
1. Try to judge the height, speed, and distance of a throw as soon as it leaves the passer's hands.
2. Make a target by cupping your hands at the spot where you would like to catch the ball.
3. As soon as you make a catch, control the ball before making the next play.
4. Make a quick stop after a catch.

As a pass is being thrown, move up and get to the ball before your opponent can steal the catch.

CATCHING DRILLS

Knowing how to catch balls is a very important part of basketball. Much patience and practice is needed in learning how to make the different catches. These drills will help you learn to catch passes.

STATIONARY CATCHES. *For one person.*
1. Hold the ball in your hands. Bounce it on the ground and catch it.
2. Toss the ball above your head, toward the front, toward the right, the left, and catch it after each toss.

PARTNER DRILLS. *For two or more players.*
1. Two players face each other about 5 yards apart.
2. They toss the ball to each other and practice catching high and low passes. In doing this drill be sure to take the proper stance as you catch each pass.

ON-THE-RUN CATCHES
1. Partners face each other about 5 yards apart.
2. One player tosses easy, slow passes toward the front, toward the right, the left, and over the head.
3. The pass receiver must run up on the ball to make these catches.

After you can do these catches well, increase the distance and speed of the throw. This will force the pass receiver to think and move more quickly.

TIMING DRILL
1. One player dribbles a short distance and quickly tosses a(n):
   a. Bounce pass
   b. Over-the-head pass
   c. Above-the-waist pass
   d. Below-the-waist pass
   e. Jump pass.
2. The other player catches each pass, then controls the ball.

This drill will help you learn to judge the

speed and movements of the player with the ball.

There is no shortcut to becoming a good player. So, don't try to learn everything at once. When you can do one drill well, try another one.

These practice drills will not only improve your playing skills but are fun to do. Enjoy your practice period and before long you will be on the way to becoming a fine player.

Chapter 9
Smart Basketball

A fine team usually plays well together. Each player knows the rules and skills of the game. They use clever strategy. This kind of team plays smart basketball!

Importance of Teamwork

Teamwork means knowing how to play well with your teammates. When there is good teamwork, each player does not try to be the hero of the game. Instead, all the players work together for the success of the team as a whole.

When you work together as a team, you can

set up smart, winning plays where everyone has a definite, important job to do. In order to have fine teamwork and use smart strategy, your team should:
1. Plan the type of defense to use against your opponents.
2. Plan the kind of offense to use.
3. Plan certain plays to be used any place on the court, especially in the scoring area.

Defensive Strategy

Do you know how to get that ball away from your opponents? How can you keep your opponents from scoring? Are you able to tell ahead of time what the other team is going to do? This is known as defensive strategy and should be planned before you go into a game. There are two kinds of defensive strategy your team may use:
1. Player-to-player defense
2. Zone defense.

The type of defense your team decides to use will depend upon:
1. The defensive skill of your players.
2. The kind of offense your opponents may use.

Choose the defense your players can do best.

Player-to-player Defense

In the player-to-player defense, each player is given the duty of guarding one opponent all

through the game wherever that opponent may go on the court. When playing on defense you must try to prevent your opponent:
1. From moving closer to the goal.
2. From passing the ball.
3. From scoring.

The best defensive player on your team usually guards the offense's best player.

SHIFTING PLAYER-TO-PLAYER DEFENSE. Sometimes during a game it becomes necessary to make a change in the player-to-player defense. For instance, you may be guarding an opponent near a spot where your teammate is guarding another player. Suddenly the player your teammate is guarding decides to move closer to you.

PLAYER-TO-PLAYER DEFENSE

WHITE—OFFENSE
DARK—DEFENSE

To avoid bumping into one another, shift smoothly and exchange guarding duties. Begin to guard your teammate's opponent and your teammate will guard your opponent until the play ends. Then you may both go back to your original guarding duties.

This is known as a shifting player-to-player defense. It takes fine teamwork to make this play work well.

Zone Defense

In the zone defense each player must guard a certain area, or zone. There are several kinds of zone defenses. Each one forms a different pattern on the court.

The zone defense is good for younger players because they do not get as tired as they would in the player-to-player defense.

TWO-THREE ZONE DEFENSE. Three players guard near the end line. They spread out and cover the area from one side line to the other. Two other players guard farther up the court. They stand, one on each side, near the free-throw jump circle.

TWO-ONE-TWO ZONE DEFENSE. Two players, one on each side, guard near the end line. The center player guards the area near the free-

throw line. Two players guard the area farther up the court, outside the free-throw jump circle.

THREE-TWO ZONE DEFENSE. The center and both forwards guard near the free-throw circle covering the area from side line to side line. Each guard protects one side of the end line, one on the left and the other on the right side.

Additional Defenses

ALL-COURT PRESS DEFENSE. When a team is losing and it is late in the game, they usually "turn on" the all-court press defense. This is a player-to-player defense but it is a stronger one because each player guards one specific opponent harder and closer. The all-court press defense works in this way:

At the instant the opposing team gets the ball, each defending player speeds toward an assigned player who must be guarded. No matter where that opponent may be on the court, the defending player sticks close and tries to force the opponent into making a bad play or losing the ball.

The suddenness of the attack and the all-out pressure on the opposing team is a very forceful play. This press defense can turn the tide from losing to winning a game.

BOXING-OUT ON REBOUND

BOXING-OUT ON THE REBOUND DEFENSE. At the moment an opponent shoots for the basket, the three players who are guarding in the area nearest the goal shift in front of the players they are guarding and "box-out" their opponents. By making this play each defensive player is now closer to the basket and has a better chance to recover the ball on the rebound.

Offensive Strategy

When a team has the ball it is in the "driver's seat," because the players have the opportunity to steer their offense into winning plays. The offense a team uses depends upon several things:
1. Condition of players.
   Are the players in good physical condition? Can they move with speed? Are they free

from worry so that they can concentrate on the game?
2. Play situations.
Are the players good at passing the ball? Can they pass and catch while on the run? Can they pivot, jump, and make hand-offs?
3. How much time is left to play?
4. What team is ahead?

The team that uses smart strategy takes all these things into account when they plan their offense.

SLOW-BREAK OFFENSE. Young players who are learning the game should start with the slow-break offense. But this does not mean that the team moves in slow motion.

In the slow break, the players move about as they pass, dribble, or hand the ball from teammate to teammate until there is a clear path to the basket. This method of moving the ball is sometimes called "weaving." There are several ways of using the slow break.

1. Your team may have no definite play in mind, but they keep weaving about on the court. They dribble and pass from one teammate to another until there is an opening toward the basket.
2. The team may weave about on the floor, passing or dribbling the ball. Then someone can throw a short pass to a player who is near the basket, who then makes the shot.
3. The pivot player or one of the taller players takes a position near the free-throw line

with his/her back toward the basket. As soon as the pivot player gets possession of the ball the very next play can be a pass, fake, hand-off play to a teammate, or shot for the basket.

Many plays can be worked out with the pivot player. But each member of the team must be ready for an opening play at the basket at all times.

FAST-BREAK OFFENSE. Use the fast-break offense if your team can move with speed and can pass and catch with accuracy while on the run. This offense works well against a team using the zone defense.

The idea of the fast break is to move the ball toward the basket before your opponents can get set to prevent the play. A fast break usually starts:
1. Right after a free throw is tried.
2. The moment a basket is made.
3. Just as a ball rebounds.

The instant one of these plays is made, make a fast break and try to keep possession of the ball. This kind of speedy play puts pressure on your opponents, because it does not give them enough time to get into their defensive positions.

Offensive Faking Plays

An alert basketball player should not only know how to shoot, dribble, and pass the ball with speed, but also know how to make fake plays. A fake play can be made with or without a ball.

In a faking play you pretend to do one thing but actually do something completely different. Because of these fake movements, your opponent becomes very confused about what is really happening.

You must be a good actor to make your faking plays look real. There are times when you use your eyes and your voice, and move your head, shoulders, arms, and feet to fool your opponent. These movements put guarding players off stride so that you can get set for a clear winning play.

FAKE DRIBBLE AND SHOOT. When you are in a close position to take a shot at the basket and an opponent is directly in front of you:

FAKE DRIBBLE AND SHOOT

1. Pivot on the right foot and make a short, quick turn toward the right.
2. Lower the ball quickly and pretend you are going to dribble toward the right. This faking movement will force your opponent to move in the direction of your imaginary dribble. Now your opponent is out of your way.
3. Quickly step back and shoot for the basket. You can make the fake dribble in any direction.

FAKE SHOT AND DRIBBLE OR PASS. If you have the ball but are not in a good shooting position because an opponent is between you and the basket:
1. Go through the motions of making a two-hand chest shot but hold on to the ball. If the faking is well done, your opponent will leap up to block the shot.
2. While the guard is off-balance, make a quick dribble, or pass the ball to a teammate who is closer to the basket.

FAKE LAY-UP SHOT AND PASS-OFF. You have dribbled close to the basket for a lay-up shot, but suddenly an opponent jumps in front to block the shot. In this case:
1. Jump up toward the basket and go through the full motion of making a lay-up shot.
2. But instead of shooting, make a quick one-hand overhead pass to a teammate. Your

FAKE LAY-UP SHOT AND PASS-OFF

teammate is now clear to make a clean shot at the basket.

Pivot Plays and Hand-offs. The pivot player is usually tall. Making passes, real and fake, making hand-offs, and shooting baskets well are the pivot player's strong game skills. For these reasons many plays take place around the pivot player, who moves about near the scoring area when the team has the ball.

Hand-off and Fake Shot. The pivot player has the ball in the free-throw-circle area, with his or her back toward the basket. With the help of a teammate, the pivot player can make a hand-off and fake shot in this way:

1. The ball is handed to a teammate who drives in toward the basket.
2. Quickly the pivot player makes a turn and fakes a hook shot at the basket.
3. In the meantime the teammate who received the ball continues to drive in with a quick dribble and then shoots for the basket.

FAKE HAND-OFF AND SHOOT. The pivot player has the ball near the free-throw-circle area. A teammate drives in close. The pivot fakes a hand-off to this teammate, then turns toward the basket and makes a nice shot at the basket.

FAKE HAND-OFF AND SHOOT

DOUBLE FAKE HAND-OFF AND SHOOT. In this play the pivot player fakes two hand-offs. One fake hand-off is made to a teammate coming in on the left and in the next motion a hand-off is faked to a teammate driving in on the right. The pivot player then turns quickly toward the basket and makes a hook shot or a one-hand jump shot.

FAKE HAND-OFF AND PASS. The pivot player is near the free-throw area. Two teammates stand several feet away.
1. The teammate on the right makes a quick run-in toward the pivot player's left side, pretends to receive a hand-off, and keeps on running.

FAKE HAND-OFF AND PASS

2. As soon as this runner has moved off, the pivot makes a quick quarter-turn toward the left and throws a soft underhand or overhead pass (whichever is better at the moment) to another teammate who has a clear path for a shot at the basket. This play can also be made toward the right.

It's fun to make these fake plays near the scoring area. But don't overdo the faking game. Learn to use fake plays only when you are in a tight spot or to get into a better scoring position. Get together with your friends and work out some fake plays of your own.

Helpful Hints
1. When playing offense keep moving to get into a clear position for the next play.
2. When playing defense learn the habits of your opponents so you will be ready to guard their moves.

SOLO PIVOT-PLAYER DRILL *With a ball.*

Take a position near the free-throw line with your back toward the basket.
1. Practice making a fake hand-off to an imaginary player, then shoot for the basket.
2. Fake a hand-off to an imaginary player, then pretend to throw a pass to another imaginary player.

DEFENSE DRILLS *For two or more players.*

Form two teams with an equal number of

players on each side. One team will play offense and the other will be on defense. Put the ball into play and see how well you can:
1. Work a player-to-player defense.
   Be sure to stick to your own opponent.
2. Try a shifting player-to-player defense.
   Can you do this without bumping into one another?
3. Practice the zone defense.
   Don't get out of your zone!

At first practice these drills in a small area on the court. When you improve, use the full court. Each team should practice both the offense and defense plays.

OFFENSE DRILLS. *For two or more players.*
1. Practice the slow-break offense.
   Don't overdo the weaving. Keep moving the ball until you can get it into a good position for a shot at the basket.
2. Try the fast break.
   Put on the speed and dribble or pass quickly to the first teammate who is free nearest the basket. Run toward the basket with full speed after you complete the pass.
3. Practice these skills:
   a. Single fake-off pass
   b. Double fake-off and dribble
   c. Single fake-off and shoot
   d. Fake shot and pass
   e. Fake dribble and shoot or pass.

PIVOT PLAYER FAKES PASS AND DRIBBLES

Using Your Basketball Notebook

1. Write down the different plays you can do well. Draw diagrams of each one.
2. Make a list of the plays you expect to use in a game. Explain each player's duties both on offense and defense. Study and try these plays one at a time.
3. When you watch your favorite teams, keep paper and pencil handy and take notes on the new plays you see.
4. Invent some new plays of your own.

It's fun to have a notebook and keep a record of the strategy plays for your team. This "paperwork" can help improve your game. Top players write, study, and learn all about the new plays before they try them out on the court.

Then in a game they use their brains and skills and play winning basketball. That's smart strategy!

Chapter 10

Getting Ready for the Big Game

Your team is now ready to play against other teams. But do you know the many things to be done before these outside games can be played?

What teams are you going to play? Where will these games take place? Do you have a captain and game officials? Do you have the proper equipment? Are your players in good physical condition?

Training Rules

Basketball is an active game and takes a great deal of energy. To keep in top physical condition obey these training rules:

PIVOT PLAYER FAKES PASS AND DRIBBLES

Using Your Basketball Notebook

1. Write down the different plays you can do well. Draw diagrams of each one.
2. Make a list of the plays you expect to use in a game. Explain each player's duties both on offense and defense. Study and try these plays one at a time.
3. When you watch your favorite teams, keep paper and pencil handy and take notes on the new plays you see.
4. Invent some new plays of your own.

It's fun to have a notebook and keep a record of the strategy plays for your team. This "paperwork" can help improve your game. Top players write, study, and learn all about the new plays before they try them out on the court.

Then in a game they use their brains and skills and play winning basketball. That's smart strategy!

Chapter 10

Getting Ready for the Big Game

Your team is now ready to play against other teams. But do you know the many things to be done before these outside games can be played?

What teams are you going to play? Where will these games take place? Do you have a captain and game officials? Do you have the proper equipment? Are your players in good physical condition?

Training Rules

Basketball is an active game and takes a great deal of energy. To keep in top physical condition obey these training rules:

1. Walk outdoors every day.

    Unglue yourself from that comfortable TV chair. Run errands for your parents and neighbors. Walk the dog. If your school is not too far, walk to school.

2. Take short runs out of doors.

    When the weather permits run short distances. Increase the distance until you can run around the block without tiring.

3. Skip rope.

    Champions follow such an exercise every day.

4. Keep your body clean.

    Use plenty of soap and water. Brush your teeth every morning and before going to bed.

5. Eat good, nourishing food every day.

    Pop, pickles, and hot dogs or hamburgers are fine for a picnic lunch but not as a daily diet. Eat meat, fruit, vegetables, cheese, eggs, and milk. These foods help the bones and muscles grow bigger and stronger.

6. Get a proper amount of sleep.

    Physically fit and alert players don't watch the late television shows.

7. Take care of cuts and bruises.

    Report them to your parents, teacher, or coach.

8. Practice the basketball skills every day.

Obey these training rules to keep in top shape. The strong and healthy player helps the team the most.

Arranging for Games

Very often a coach makes the arrangements for games, but if the coach is too busy your captain or a committee may take over these duties.

First, your game committee will have to find teams to play against. The way to do this is to phone, write, or visit the captain or coach of other teams and ask for games.

Then there are certain details that should be discussed. Are the teams evenly matched as to size and playing ability? Is a playing court available? Is this court marked, and does it have the proper equipment? Is it a safe place for players and fans?

Before making the final arrangements be sure to get the approval of your coach. Then set the date for each of the games you expect to play.

Where to Play

A committee may be appointed to find a playing court. This committee can check the gymnasiums that have indoor basketball courts at the neighborhood schools, YMCA's, settlement houses, parks, and Boy's and Girl's Clubs.

Many boys and girls play some form of basketball outdoors. For these games it is not necessary to have the full field equipment that is needed for regular indoor games.

Official Measurements for Young Players' Courts

The size of your basketball court is decided by the neighborhood facilities that are available and the league or associations sponsoring the games.

Youth Basketball Association (YBA) games are played on courts from a minimum of 60 feet long and 40 feet wide to a maximum of 84 feet long and 50 feet wide. The free-throw line is reduced to 12 feet from the backboard, for players on the 3rd- and 4th-grade teams. Teams beyond the 5th grade use the regular 15-foot foul line. All other dimensions follow the rules of the National Federation of State High School Associations.

Biddy Basketball games are played on a court 60 feet long and 40 feet wide. The

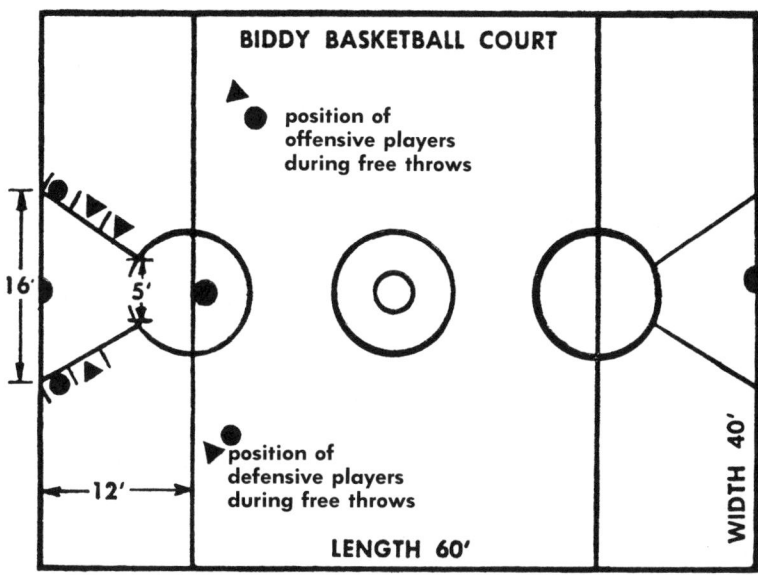

outside center-jump circle and the free-throw circles are 5 feet in diameter (width) instead of the regular 6 feet.

Beginning at each end of the free-throw circle are two lines, 5 feet apart, which stretch diagonally outward toward the end lines to a distance of 16 feet apart. These are the *free-throw-lane lines*. The space between the free-throw-lane lines is called the "key lock" area because it looks like a keyhole. The lane lines are divided into three parts by 8-inch markings. These marks show where the players stand when a free throw is made.

Equipment

The supplies used on the court are called "field equipment." The uniforms and other articles used by players and officials are called "personal equipment."

Field Equipment

The field equipment includes the backboards, baskets, officials' table, players' benches, scoreboard, loudspeakers, and the officials' bell, siren, horn, and pistol.

THE BACKBOARD. The regular rectangular board is 6 feet long and 4 feet wide, while the fan-shaped is 54 inches long and 35 inches

BASKETBALL BACKBOARDS

WOOD

GLASS RECTANGULAR

STEEL FAN-SHAPED

GLASS FAN-SHAPED

high. The Biddy Basketball backboard is 4 feet long and 3 feet high.

BASKET RING AND NET. The basket ring, or hoop, is 17 inches in diameter for Biddy Basketball and 18 inches for Youth Basketball Association (YBA) games. It is attached to the backboard $8^1/_2$ feet above the ground. YBA players in the 5th grade and beyond use the regular 10-foot basket ring height. The net is made of cord and is fastened to the basket ring.

OFFICIALS' TABLE. This table stands at least 3 feet outside the side lines at the center of the court, for the use of the officials.

PLAYERS' BENCHES. A players' bench is placed at either side of the officials' table.

SCOREBOARD. At one end of the court is a large scoreboard that helps the fans follow the game.

LOUDSPEAKERS. These are placed in different parts of the gymnasium so that all fans can hear the announcer.

Young Players' Personal Equipment

In league games each player has two complete uniforms. One is light in color and the other is dark. When a team plays upon the home court they wear their light uniforms and for games away from home they wear the dark suits. In this way the two teams playing against each other never wear the same colors.

To enjoy the game all you need is a basketball, sneakers, and play clothes. But for your regular games your team may wish to buy regular uniforms.

The regular uniform consists of pants, jersey, socks or stockings, shoes, warm-up suits, knee and elbow pads, eyeglass protectors, and the ball.

SHIRTS. The shirt or jersey may be sleeveless or have short sleeves. Shirts may be bought in the school or team colors. The player's number should be stitched on the back, with the name of the team, letter, or number on the front of the jersey.

PANTS. The pants come in two styles, the boxer type or half-belt style. These pants may

FULL DRESS UNIFORM

be of any color the team chooses. Some girls' teams wear a short skirt.

SHOES. The shoes must have rubber soles. They may lace above the ankles or you may wear the oxford style.

SOCKS AND STOCKINGS. Heavy sweat socks are best. Some teams wear longer stockings that reach just below the knees. These are held in place by an elastic band.

WARM-UP SUITS. Before a game the players wear a jacket or long shirt and long pants over their uniforms. These "warm-up" suits are worn when the players are not taking part in the actual game.

KNEE AND ELBOW PADS. Players may wear knee and elbow pads for protection. These are rubber pads covered with elastic cloth.

EYEGLASS PROTECTORS. Players who wear glasses may use special eyeglass protectors. These are lightweight steel or plastic frames, which are placed over the eyeglasses to keep them from falling off or breaking.

OFFICIAL BALL. The ball may be made of leather or rubber. Your official ball must be 28 inches in circumference, which is the measurement around the widest part.

All this personal equipment may be bought in sporting goods stores or from athletic equipment companies.

Officials' Personal Equipment

An official must wear a uniform, too. Each game official wears a black-and-white striped shirt, either light or dark trousers, sweat socks, and rubber-soled shoes.

The *referee* and the *umpire* carry a whistle and a rule book. The *scorekeepers* are supplied with a horn, pencil, paper, and scoresheets. The *timekeepers* have a stopwatch and gong, pistol, or siren.

How to Get Uniforms

Uniforms are expensive. Some teams have organizations that sponsor them and buy the equipment. But if you don't have a sponsor, there are many ways to earn money to buy your personal equipment.

Working As a Team

Whether you work alone or as a team, you can do a good turn and help your neighborhood.

PAPER DRIVE. Conduct a paper drive in your community. All the members of the team can collect papers and old magazines and sell them to dealers.

ORGANIZE A CLEAN-UP DRIVE. Offer to clean yards, sweep sidewalks, cut and water the lawns, rake the grass. You can trim hedges and pull weeds.

SHOPPER'S DELIVERY SERVICE. Organize a delivery service. Help the shoppers with their packages.

PLAYS, PUPPET SHOWS, AND MAGIC SHOWS. These shows can be given either inside or out of doors. Dramatize one of your favorite stories in the form of a play or puppet show. If someone on your team is a clever magician, put on a magic show. This is fun!

Working Alone

Anyone who is working alone can always run errands, deliver newspapers, or collect old newspapers, used bottles, or scrap metals.

Learn to make things. Join an arts-and-crafts class at your neighborhood park, settlement house, YWCA or YMCA. Make birdhouses and feeders, fish flies, ash trays, and toys.

Make enameled pins and earrings for women, and cuff links and tie clasps for men.

Get some practical use out of your camera. Learn to take pictures of babies and little children. Parents are always ready to buy good pictures of their children.

If you live in the country, there is always the job of pulling weeds and picking berries. Gather and candle eggs, tend and feed the farm animals, herd sheep or cattle, and clean barns.

Keep your eyes and ears open and give help where it is needed.

Be sure to get permission of your parents or

guardian before setting out on any of these projects.

Team Secretary

Your team should elect or choose a secretary. This person will keep a record of the games, players, equipment, and when and where the games will be played. The secretary will give this information to the team before every game so they will know what to expect when they meet their opponents.

Team Captain

The team should elect a captain to represent them. The captain is the only player who speaks for the team when there is any complaint to be made to the officials.

Your captain should like the game, know the rules, be able to get along with people, and be respected and liked by the members of the team.

Coach

An older person should serve as coach. It's important that this person know the game well, enjoy working with young people, and be able to teach the many skills during practice periods. The coach decides upon the starting line-up, sends in the substitutes, and gives advice all through the game.

Game Officials

If possible try to have regular game officials. They keep the action moving according to the rules and your game will go along smoothly.

For important games the officials are the referee and the umpire, two timekeepers, and two scorers. If you wish, your games may be played with one referee, one timekeeper, and one scorekeeper.

REFEREE AND UMPIRE. If you have both a *referee* and *umpire*, each one covers a certain part of the court to see that the game is played according to the rules. In the case of any argument or disagreement upon the court the referee makes the final decision.

If only one official is used s/he is called the referee and takes complete charge of the game. Any parent, teacher, or player can buy an official rulebook at a sporting goods store.

SCOREKEEPER. An adult or young person may be chosen as the scorekeeper. The scorekeeper may choose an assistant for help. The scorekeeper should know the game, watch carefully, and keep a correct record of the scores made by both teams and players.

TIMEKEEPER. A grownup or young friend may serve as timekeeper. An assistant is chosen if necessary. The timekeeper must keep a careful check of the actual playing time and time-outs.

In a regular game the timekeeper sounds a gong, pistol, or siren to notify the referee when to start each period of play, when each period ends, and when each time-out period ends. The timekeeper may also operate the electric scoreboard if there is one.

ANNOUNCER. Perhaps you will also have an announcer call out the names of the starting players and substitutes. This official tells the fans something about the height, weight, and playing records of the teams and players. The announcer adds to the enjoyment of the game by giving a running account of the highlights as they take place on the court. The game officials sit at the officials' table. Of course the referee and umpire do their work out on the court.

The Game Begins

Before the game, the coach and captains of each team get together with the referee to choose goals. The referee tosses a coin while the captains yell "Heads!" or "Tails!" The team that wins the toss chooses the goal they wish to defend. No matter who wins the toss, both teams change goals at the end of the first half.

When the big moment comes and both teams run out onto the court and the game begins, you can be proud of the part you played in making it possible for your team to play against another team.

Youth Basketball Playing Rules

AGE AND HEIGHT OF PLAYERS. *Biddy Basketball League* players must be between nine and twelve years of age. No player may be over 5 feet 6 inches tall at the beginning of the season.

Youth Basketball Association players are asked to compete with boys and girls of their own age or grade in school. Teams are allowed to have 3rd and 4th graders on one team, 5th and 6th graders on another team, and so on up through 11th and 12th graders. Leagues may organize teams for all boys, all girls, or boys and girls on the same team.

LENGTH OF GAME. For Biddy Basketball and YBA games the actual playing time is twenty-four minutes. The game is divided into four quarters of six minutes each. There is a two-minute rest period at the end of the first and third quarters. During the half-time period, the YBA teams must have at least a three-minute to ten-minute rest period and the Biddy Basketball players must have a ten-minute rest.

If the score is a tie at the end of the fourth quarter, both teams must play an extra two-minute period. They will play as many extra two-minute periods as are necessary to break the tie.

PLAYER'S PLAYING TIME. For Biddy Basketball there should be at least ten players in uniform for each team. Every player in uniform will have the opportunity to play at least six minutes during a game.

A YBA team is usually made up of nine players. They all get a chance to play at least one quarter (six minutes) in each game. No player is allowed to play the whole game. This rule gives every boy and girl an equal chance to play and have fun.

Position of Players

DURING A FREE-THROW SHOT. There is a definite rule that tells where players should stand during a free-throw shot.

For Biddy Basketball:
1. The shooter must stand with toes just behind the free-throw line before making the shot.
2. Two teammates take their positions next to the backboard, one on each side of the foul-lane line.
3. Two more teammates stand behind the foul line, one on each side of the court.

The opposing players take these positions:
1. One stands on the left lane line next to the player who is near the backboard.
2. Two players stand on the right lane line next to the player who is near the backboard.
3. Two stand behind the free-throw line, one on each side near the offensive players.

For Youth Basketball Association:
1. The shooter stands with toes behind the free-throw line before trying the shot.
2. Two opponents take their positions nearest to the backboard, one on each side of the foul-lane line.
3. Two teammates take their positions next to the players who are near the backboard.
4. Two opposing players may stand in the third foul-lane space away from the basket.
5. Two teammates may stand in the fourth foul-lane space away from the basket.
6. One opposing player stands well behind the free-throw line. A teammate also has the choice of taking a position away from the players' foul-lane space.

Additional Rules and Penalties

FOULS. The player who makes a foul must raise one arm high in the air so the scorer can see the number on the jersey and mark it on the official scoresheet. After six personal fouls, the player must leave the game.

TIME-OUTS. Each team is allowed five time-outs during a game. A team is permitted to have one time-out for each extra two-minute overtime period of play.

Unsportsmanlike Play

1. Any player who disobeys the officials must leave the game.
2. Any player who hits, kicks, or uses rough language must leave the game.

SUBSTITUTES. Five players from each team are allowed to play on the court at one time. Before going into the game to replace a teammate, the substitute must report to the official scorers and give name, number, and playing position.

"Little-Guys" and "Little-Gals" Game

This game is for young boys and girls between nine and twelve years of age who are five feet tall or under. The playing rules are just the same as for Biddy Basketball and the YBA.

So, if you are not so tall, don't let that stop you from playing. But be sure to play with teammates and friends of your own size and playing ability.

Remember, even though the game for younger players is shorter and some rules may be a little different from those used by bigger and more experienced players, the skills of the game are the same ones the top players use.

Whether you are short or tall, boy or girl, basketball is fun for everyone. So, get out and play and enjoy the game!

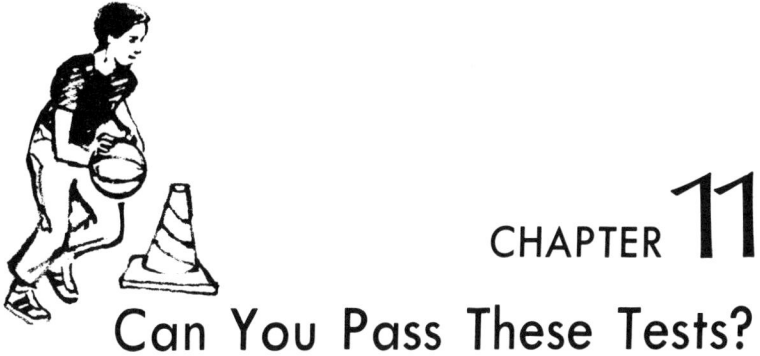

CHAPTER 11

Can You Pass These Tests?

There are many kinds of tests given by a doctor and at school. You will be taking them from the time you are young until the time you become quite old. Doctors give you tests to measure your health. In school your teachers give tests to find out how well you understand your subjects. Your physical education teacher and coach give physical fitness and sports skill tests.

Basketball Tests

What are some of the basketball tests that young boys and girls can take? Coaches on college and professional teams give very rigid basketball tests. Many teachers and coaches of youth clubs and school teams also give special basketball tests. Here is one of the most popular for young players.

BASKETBALL SKILLS TEST. The American Alliance for Health, Physical Education, and Recreation (AAHPER) in Washington, D.C., prepared a test that will show how you rate in basketball. It is known as the *AAHPER Basketball Skills Test.* This test has been given to thousands of youngsters in the United States of America to measure their basketball skills in nine different events.*

Rules for Taking Basketball Test

1. This test is for boys and girls from ten to eighteen years of age.
2. You may take the test indoors or outdoors.
3. If you are under ten years of age *do not* try to keep up with scores of older players. Use the test as a practice drill.
4. Tests may be taken in any numbered order you wish.
5. Take a short warm-up before taking the test.

*Reprinted (with changes) from Basketball Skills Test Manual, 1966 with permission of the American Alliance for Health, Physical Education, and Recreation, 1201 Sixteenth Street, N.W., Washington, D.C. 20036.

6. You are allowed at least one but no more than two practice tries for each event before taking the test.
7. Wear sneakers, jersey or sweatsuit, dungarees, or gym suit.
8. If you are in condition and have time, complete the tests in one day. If you take the test on two separate days, divide the test into two parts.
9. Have a partner help you to keep score and to retrieve loose balls.

FIRST DAY	SECOND DAY
1. Front Shot	6. Jump and Reach
2. Side Shot	7. Overarm Pass for Accuracy
3. Foul Shot	
4. Under Basket Shot	8. Push Pass for Accuracy
5. Speed Pass	9. Dribbling

How Will You Rate? If you do poorly in "dribbling while on the run" you may have a hard time dodging players. If you have weak arms and hands, the shot for the basket may be hard to do. This means that you should practice more agility, change-of-direction running, and arm- and hand-strengthening exercises.

The way you rate in this test will help you find out your strong and weak points. If you show weaknesses in some basketball skills, work to improve. But if you make a good rating, hold on to your strong points by keeping up with your exercises and game skills.

AAHPER Basketball Skills Tests

Front Shot (Boys and Girls)

This test measures your accuracy in making successful shots at the basket from a position in front of the basket.

a. Have a basketball and take a position just behind the left side of the free-throw circle where the free-throw line crosses the circle. Draw a mark on this spot.
b. Take a position on this spot and try to make the ball go into the basket without hitting the backboard. You are allowed to take any type of shot using one or two hands.
c. You have *fifteen tries* to make a basket. After every series of five shots you must leave your "spot" on the floor before starting on your next series of five shots.

You get *two points* for each basket made, even if the ball hits the backboard or rim first. *One point* is counted for shots that hit the rim but do not go into the basket. However, no points are counted if the ball hits the backboard before it touches the rim. No points are counted for balls that hit the backboard and do

FRONT SHOT (BOYS)

Age	10	11	12	13	14	15	16	17–18
Rating				*Number of Points*				
Superior	23	26	27	27	27	29	29	30
Excellent	12	14	16	17	19	20	20	20
Good	9	11	13	15	16	17	17	17
Satisfactory	6	8	10	12	14	15	15	15
Poor	3	5	7	10	11	12	12	12

not go into the basket. Add the total points made for the fifteen shots. This is your score.

KEY TO SCORE: Your rating is based on your age and the points you receive for scoring baskets. The numbers on the chart show the total points you should get for each age.

AGE: Find your age in the top row.

NUMBER OF POINTS: Locate the number of points you scored in the column below your age.

RATING: Check the number of points you made and find your rating in the left-hand column.

EXAMPLE: If you are a ten-year-old boy and scored twelve points, your rating is *excellent.*

If you are ten years old and scored nine points, your rating is *good.* If you got more than nine points but less than twelve points, your rating remains good but it is closer to excellent.

FRONT SHOT (GIRLS)

Age	10–11	12	13	14	15	16	17–18
Rating			*Number of Points*				
Superior	21	21	30	30	30	30	30
Excellent	10	11	13	14	14	14	15
Good	6	8	9	10	11	12	12
Satisfactory	3	6	6	8	8	9	9
Poor	1	3	4	4	5	6	6

Side Shot (Boys and Girls)

This test measures your accuracy in making shots at the basket from a spot at the side of the basket.

a. Mark a spot located near each corner of the basketball court. *Boys'* markers measure twenty feet from the center of the basket rim. *Girls'* markers should be fifteen feet from the center of the rim. The marks must "line up" evenly with the side of the basket.
b. Take a position on one of the markers and try to shoot the ball into the basket. You have *ten tries*.
c. Move to the marker on the other side of the court and take another *ten tries* to make a basket.

Count *two points* for each basket made and *one point* for balls that hit the basket rim but do not go in. Points are allowed even when the ball hits the backboard. Forty points is the highest score possible. Make a record of your score.

SIDE SHOT (BOYS)

Age	10	11	12	13	14	15	16	17–18
Rating				Number of Points				
Superior	27	29	32	33	35	35	35	36
Excellent	11	13	17	19	21	21	21	22
Good	6	9	12	14	17	17	17	19
Satisfactory	3	5	9	11	15	15	15	16
Poor	1	2	5	7	11	11	11	12

KEY: Your rating is measured by the number of points you receive for scoring baskets. The numbers on the chart show the total points you should get for each age.

SIDE SHOT (GIRLS)

Age	10–11	12	13	14	15	16	17–18
Rating			Number of Points				
Superior	25	26	29	30	31	31	32
Excellent	11	12	14	16	17	17	17
Good	6	8	11	12	13	13	13
Satisfactory	3	5	7	9	10	10	10
Poor	0	2	4	6	6	6	6

Foul Shots (Boys and Girls)

This test measures your accuracy in making free throws. A partner should help to keep score and retrieve loose balls.

a. Take a position behind the center of the free-throw line.
b. You have *twenty tries* to make as many free throws as possible. After every series of five shots you must leave your "spot" on the floor momentarily before starting on the next series of five free throws.
c. You may use any of your favorite shots— one-hand, two-hand, underhand or overhead.

One point is counted for each goal made regardless of how the ball goes into the basket. This is your total score.

FOUL SHOT (BOYS)

Age	10	11	12	13	14	15	16	17–18
Rating				Number of Baskets				
Superior	13	16	17	20	20	20	20	20
Excellent	4	5	7	8	10	11	11	11
Good	2	3	5	6	7	8	8	8
Satisfactory	1	2	3	4	5	7	7	7
Poor	0	1	2	2	4	4	4	4

FOUL SHOT (GIRLS)

Age	10-11	12	13	14	15	16	17-18
Rating			Number of Baskets				
Superior	20	20	20	20	20	20	20
Excellent	4	5	5	5	6	7	7
Good	2	3	3	3	4	5	5
Satisfactory	1	2	2	2	3	3	4
Poor	0	1	1	1	2	2	2

Under Basket Shot (Boys and Girls)

This test measures your speed and accuracy in making rapid shots at the basket from a position under the basket.

a. Hold a basketball directly under the basket.
b. When your partner with a stopwatch signals "go," start making one-hand or two-hand lay-up shots, recover the ball, and shoot again as rapidly as possible.
c. Try to make as many goals as possible within 30 seconds when your partner signals "stop."
d. You have two trials of 30-second periods.

One point is scored for each basket made. Your score is the number of baskets made in 30 seconds. Take the best score of the two trials.

UNDER BASKET SHOT (BOYS)

Age	10	11	12	13	14	15	16	17-18
Rating	Number of Baskets Made in Thirty Seconds							
Superior	14	23	23	23	23	29	33	34
Excellent	7	8	10	12	14	15	15	16
Good	5	6	8	9	11	13	13	14
Satisfactory	4	5	5	6	9	10	11	11
Poor	3	3	4	5	7	8	8	9

UNDER BASKET SHOT (GIRLS)

Age	10–11	12	13	14	15	16	17–18
Rating	*Number of Baskets Made in Thirty Seconds*						
Superior	15	15	16	16	18	19	20
Excellent	5	7	7	8	8	9	9
Good	4	5	6	6	6	7	7
Satisfactory	3	4	5	5	5	5	5
Poor	2	3	3	4	4	4	4

Speed Pass (Boys and Girls)

This test measures the speed at which you can continue to pass or catch a basketball.

a. Locate a level floor or ground and a wall with a smooth surface.

b. Take a position behind a line you have marked 9 feet from the smooth, solid wall.

c. On your partner's signal "go," start passing the ball against the wall, *catch* the rebound, and continue *passing* against the wall as rapidly as possible until *ten passes* have hit the wall.

d. Head-high passes against the wall are best; and push passes are faster.

e. You have two trials.

Your score is the best time required to complete ten passes against the wall. The stopwatch is started when the first pass hits the wall and stopped when the tenth pass hits the wall. All passes must begin from behind the line. Mark down the time for your fastest trial for making ten passes. Locate your score.

SPEED PASS (BOYS)

Age	10	11	12	13	14	15	16	17–18
Rating	Time in Seconds and Tenths of Seconds							
Superior	10.0	8.5	5.5	5.5	5.5	4.5	4.5	4.5
Excellent	12.5	11.9	10.4	9.3	8.6	8.3	8.1	7.8
Good	13.6	12.9	11.7	10.6	9.4	9.1	8.9	8.6
Satisfactory	14.9	14.0	12.7	11.8	10.4	10.0	9.6	9.4
Poor	16.5	15.3	14.2	13.4	11.7	11.3	11.1	10.5

KEY TO MEASURE SPEED-PASSING TIME: The number to the left of the decimal point is *seconds*. The number to the right of the decimal is *tenths of a second*.

EXAMPLE: If you are an 11-year-old girl and made ten passes against the wall in *twelve and nine-tenths seconds,* your rating is *superior.*

SPEED PASS (GIRLS)

Age	10–11	12	13	14	15	16	17–18
Rating	Time in Seconds and Tenths of Seconds						
Superior	7.5	7.5	7.5	7.5	7.5	6.5	6.5
Excellent	13.2	12.0	12.0	11.5	11.0	10.9	10.7
Good	14.5	13.4	13.2	12.7	12.2	12.1	11.9
Satisfactory	15.9	14.8	14.5	14.0	13.5	13.4	13.1
Poor	17.7	16.8	16.4	15.5	15.3	15.1	15.0

Jump and Reach (Boys and Girls)

This test measures the height you can jump over and above your reach from a standing-still position. (This is also known as leg-explosive power.)

Attach a large piece of clear wrapping paper, cardboard, or canvas to a smooth wall with a level floor below. (An old piece of blackboard is best if you can find one.) The "jump and reach" target should be attached to the wall so the bottom end is within the standing-still reach of the smallest player.

a. Hold a small piece of chalk in your fingers. Stand close to the wall with the side that has the chalk in your hand. Keep knees straight and feet flat on the floor.
b. *Reach* (stretch) up as far as possible and make a mark on the target at the very top of your reach.
c. Start crouching and swinging your arms up and down, then *jump* as high as possible. Quickly make a second mark on the wall target.
d. With a yardstick, measure the distance between the top of the reach (first) and top of the jump (second) marks on the target.
e. The distance between these two marks is your score. Your final score is the best of two trials.

JUMP AND REACH (BOYS)

Age	10	11	12	13	14	15	16	17–18
Rating				*Inches*				
Superior	18	22	25	29	29	31	31	34
Excellent	12	14	16	17	20	21	21	24
Good	11	12	14	16	18	19	20	22
Satisfactory	10	11	13	14	16	17	18	19
Poor	9	9	10	11	13	14	15	16

KEY: The jump and reach skill is scored by measuring the distance between your standing-reach height and your jumping height. The numbers on the chart show in inches what the jump and reach distance should be for each age.

JUMP AND REACH (GIRLS)

Age	10–11	12	13	14	15	16	17–18
Rating				Inches			
Superior	18	21	24	24	25	25	25
Excellent	12	14	15	15	16	16	16
Good	11	12	13	13	14	14	14
Satisfactory	10	11	11	12	13	13	13
Poor	9	9	10	10	11	11	11

Overarm Pass for Accuracy (Boys and Girls)

This test measures your accuracy in making a one-hand overarm pass at a stationary target.

Take a five-foot by five-foot piece of canvas, wrapping paper, cardboard, or cloth. Mark three circles on the canvas. Make a circle *eighteen inches* in diameter in the center of the canvas, a *thirty-eight inch* middle circle around it, and a *fifty-eight inch* outer circle. Make the circle lines thick enough so you can see them from a short distance. Hang the canvas target on a smooth wall. The bottom of the outer fifty-eight inch circle must be three feet above the ground. Now mark a long *throwing line* thirty-five feet from the target for boys and twenty feet for girls.

a. Take a passer's position one step behind the throwing line and face the center target.

b. Start by holding the basketball in two hands. Take a short step forward and throw a one-hand overarm "bullseye" pass at the target. You must not step beyond the line.

You have ten chances to pass toward the target. You get *three points* for hitting the line or inside of the center circle, *two points* for hitting the line or inside of the middle circle, and *one point* for hitting the line or inside of the outer circle. Add the total points made for the ten throws. This is your score.

OVERARM PASS FOR ACCURACY (BOYS)

Age	10	11	12	13	14	15	16	17–18
Rating				*Number of Points*				
Superior	18	27	27	27	29	31	31	31
Excellent	10	12	16	17	19	20	20	21
Good	6	9	12	15	17	17	17	17
Satisfactory	2	5	10	12	14	15	15	15
Poor	0	2	6	9	10	11	11	11

OVERARM PASS FOR ACCURACY (GIRLS)

Age	10–11	12	13	14	15	16	17–18
Rating				*Number of Points*			
Superior	27	29	30	30	30	30	30
Excellent	19	21	22	22	23	23	23
Good	14	17	18	19	20	21	20
Satisfactory	10	14	15	16	17	17	17
Poor	4	9	11	13	13	14	11

Push Pass for Accuracy (Boys and Girls)

This test measures your accuracy in making a two-hand push (chest) pass at a stationary target.

Use the same target as in the one-hand

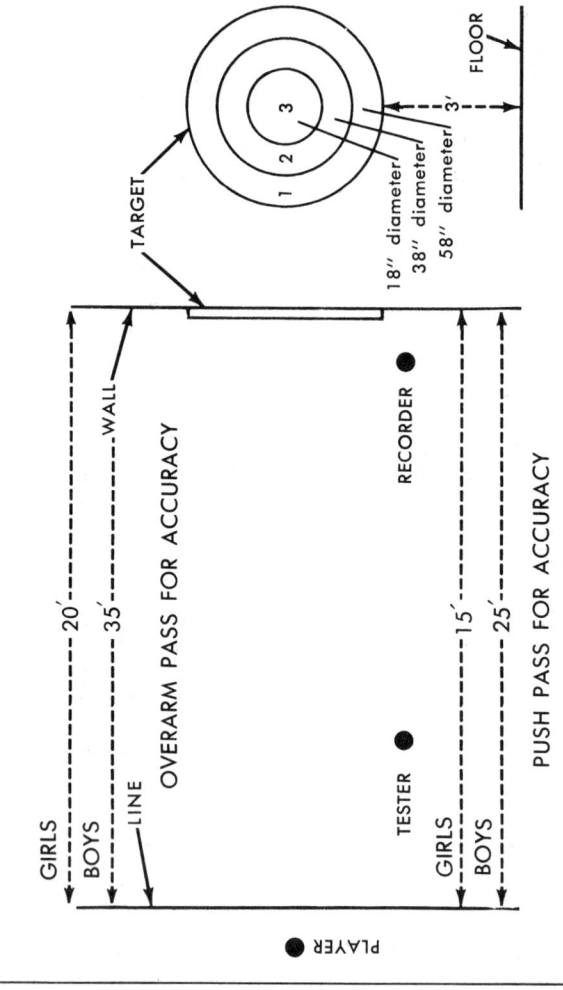

b. Start by holding the basketball in two hands. Take a short step forward and throw a one-hand overarm "bullseye" pass at the target. You must not step beyond the line.

You have ten chances to pass toward the target. You get *three points* for hitting the line or inside of the center circle, *two points* for hitting the line or inside of the middle circle, and *one point* for hitting the line or inside of the outer circle. Add the total points made for the ten throws. This is your score.

OVERARM PASS FOR ACCURACY (BOYS)

Age	10	11	12	13	14	15	16	17–18
Rating				*Number of Points*				
Superior	18	27	27	27	29	31	31	31
Excellent	10	12	16	17	19	20	20	21
Good	6	9	12	15	17	17	17	17
Satisfactory	2	5	10	12	14	15	15	15
Poor	0	2	6	9	10	11	11	11

OVERARM PASS FOR ACCURACY (GIRLS)

Age	10–11	12	13	14	15	16	17–18
Rating			*Number of Points*				
Superior	27	29	30	30	30	30	30
Excellent	19	21	22	22	23	23	23
Good	14	17	18	19	20	21	20
Satisfactory	10	14	15	16	17	17	17
Poor	4	9	11	13	13	14	11

Push Pass for Accuracy (Boys and Girls)

This test measures your accuracy in making a two-hand push (chest) pass at a stationary target.

Use the same target as in the one-hand

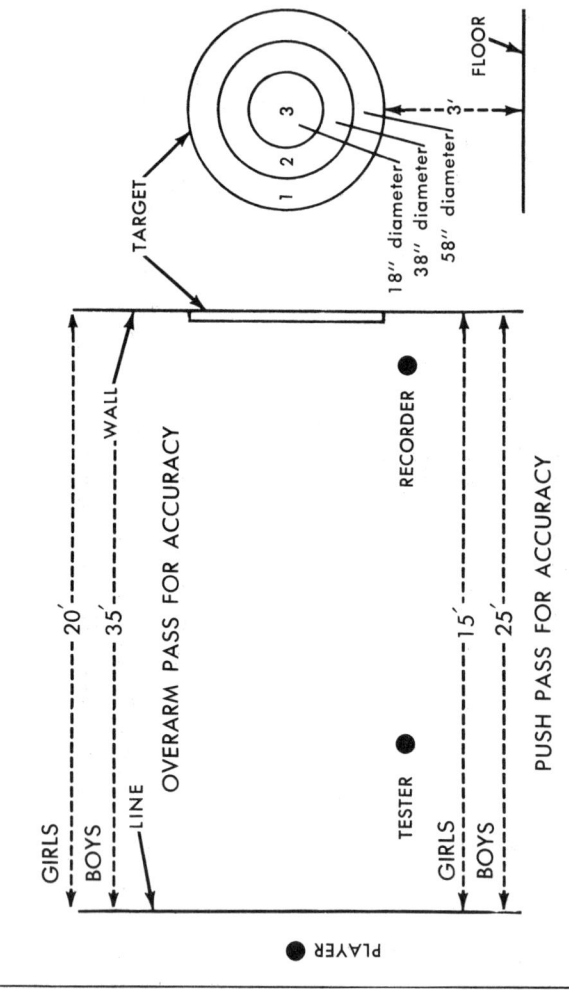

overarm pass. Mark a long *throwing line* twenty-five feet from the target for boys and fifteen feet for girls.

a. Stand behind the throwing line facing the target.
b. Take your favorite two-hand push-pass grip on the basketball.
c. Make a "snappy" push pass, aiming for the center "bullseye." Keep both feet behind the line.

You have ten chances to pass toward the target. You get *three points* for hitting the line or inside of the center circle, *two points* for hitting the line or inside of the middle circle, and *one point* for hitting the line or inside of

PUSH PASS FOR ACCURACY (BOYS)

Age	11	12	13	14	15	16	17–18
Rating			*Number of Points*				
Superior	29	29	29	29	29	30	30
Excellent	12	16	20	21	23	24	27
Good	7	11	16	18	21	21	26
Satisfactory	2	7	12	15	18	18	23
Poor	1	2	7	11	14	15	20

PUSH PASS FOR ACCURACY (GIRLS)

Age	10–11	12	13	14	15	16	17–18
Rating			*Number of Points*				
Superior	29	30	30	30	30	30	30
Excellent	22	24	25	26	27	27	27
Good	19	21	22	23	24	25	25
Satisfactory	15	18	20	21	22	22	23
Poor	8	12	15	17	19	19	19

the outer circle. Add the total points made for the ten passes. Thirty points is a perfect score.

Dribble (Boys and Girls)

This test measures your speed in the "zig-zag" running dribble.

Mark a starting line on the ground. Have six old chairs ready. Arrange the chairs in a straight line with the first chair five feet away from the starting line. Place the remaining chairs eight feet apart farther on. The last chair is now forty-five feet from the starting line. Face the sitting portion of the chairs away from the line. If you don't have chairs, use rubber cones, stools, bundles of newspapers, or magazines stacked to the height of a chair.

Get into position behind the starting line, a little to the right of the first chair, with a basketball in your favorite dribbling hand. Have a partner with a stopwatch to check your running dribble time.

a. On the word "go" dribble around the right of the *first chair* and quickly start to shift the dribbling to your left.
b. Dribble around the left of the *second chair*, while continuing to shift your dribble to the right.
c. Continue to *dribble in and out around each chair.*
d. Circle around the last chair and continue the running dribble in-and-out around the chairs on your way back to the starting line.

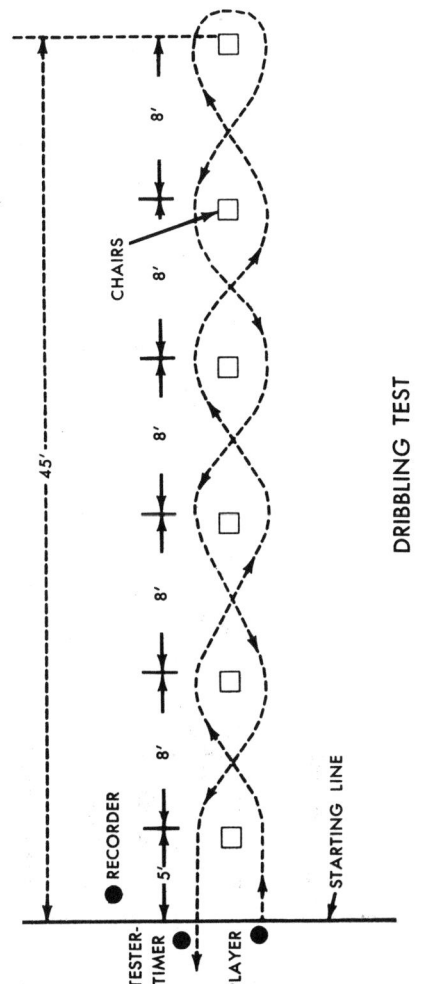

You have two trials. The ball may be dribbled with either hand. Record the best running-dribble time from the word "go" to when you cross the line. Remember: the ball must be dribbled at least once after you pass each chair, but need not be dribbled when you are opposite a chair. *You must not hit the chairs.*

DRIBBLING (BOYS)

Age	10	11	12	13	14	15	16	17–18
Rating	*Time in Seconds and Tenths of Seconds*							
Superior	12.0	10.5	6.5	6.5	6.5	5.5	5.5	5.5
Excellent	14.6	13.3	12.2	11.2	10.9	10.3	10.3	10.3
Good	15.5	14.4	13.2	12.4	11.8	11.4	11.3	11.2
Satisfactory	16.5	15.6	14.4	13.6	12.9	12.6	12.3	12.0
Poor	18.0	17.2	15.8	14.9	14.3	14.5	13.4	13.3

KEY: The zigzag running-dribble time is measured in seconds and tenths of seconds. The numbers on the chart show the time the dribbling should take for each age.

DRIBBLING (GIRLS)

Age	10–11	12	13	14	15	16	17–18
Rating	*Time in Seconds and Tenths of Seconds*						
Superior	9.5	9.5	9.5	9.5	9.5	8.5	7.5
Excellent	15.2	14.0	13.7	13.4	13.1	12.5	12.4
Good	16.5	15.2	14.9	14.5	14.0	13.5	13.4
Satisfactory	17.8	16.5	16.1	15.5	15.0	14.6	14.5
Poor	19.5	18.2	17.5	17.0	16.3	16.0	15.5

What Is Your Final Score?

Were you satisfied with your rating? If not, ask yourself these questions:

1. Do you use the right *body movements* for the different basketball skills? Do you use your muscles often enough to develop and improve these movement skills?
2. Do you take part *steadily* in games and practice drills? Or do you let your muscles become flabby?
3. Do you watch your weight? If you are overweight or underweight you must watch the kind and amount of food you eat.
4. Do you feel alert and well? If you "huff and puff" when you work or play, you should go to your doctor for a health checkup.

For a Better Score

Any of the reasons above could be the cause of a poor showing on the basketball tests. This means that you should plan for regular workouts.

MAKE YOUR WORKOUTS FUN. Do them with friends. Get help from teachers and coaches. Try them with your family and relatives. Don't become discouraged if you didn't do well. It's more important to improve slowly and at the same time enjoy the basketball fun. If your test score is excellent, hold on to it with regular workouts.

Now review the different skills the players on a basketball team must have. Study them! Practice them!

Chapter 12

Scores and Records

During a game the official scorekeeper gives all members of the team grades on their playing ability. These grades measure everything the player did on the basketball court.

How many baskets did the player shoot? How many fouls did the player make? Did the player play well with teammates? All this information and much more is put down on the scorekeeper's records for all the official games played during the season.

The Scorekeepers

When big-league teams play a game, they use two scorekeepers. The home team provides the official scorekeeper and the visiting team furnishes the assistant. These two scorekeepers know the rules of the game and they understand the work of each player.

During a game both scorekeepers sit at the officials' table with scoresheets, pencils, and paper. They watch the game carefully. They fill in the scoresheets, make a report on the games, and also answer other questions about the players and the team as a whole.

They send their official scores and reports to the Commissioner of the Conference, where they are filed away and kept as lasting records.

Sportswriters and radio and television announcers also follow the game and keep records of their own.

Team Records

There is no set rule as to the kinds of records to be kept, but certain information is needed to figure out the team and player standings. The official scorekeeper fills out a team record, which answers these questions:
1. The name of both teams.
2. When and where the game was played.
3. Names of the officials.
4. Names of players for both teams.
5. Length of game.
6. Number of points made by each team.

7. How the players scored their points.
8. Number of fouls made by each team.
9. Number of time-outs taken by each team.

Player Records

Some of the more important questions a scorekeeper answers about each player are:
1. Name, number, and position of each player in the starting line-up.
2. Name of every substitute who entered the game.
3. Number of minutes each player was in the game.
4. Number of fouls each player made.
5. Number of field-goal shots attempted and missed.
6. Number of field goals and free throws each player made.
7. Number of free-throw shots attempted and missed.
8. Number of rebounds caught on offense and defense.
9. Number of times a player assisted teammates in making a score.

These records really go into detail but this is not all. There are even more kinds of information that go into the records.

Team Scorekeeper

A student who is the team manager also keeps score at every game. In addition, the

team manager fills out a detailed report on each player and answers such questions as these:
1. Did player play a steady game?
2. Did player score with shots from the side line, middle-court area, or by making free throws?
3. Was scoring made through jump shots, two-handed push shots, or pivot shots?
4. Did player guard well?
5. Did player show good teamwork?
6. How many points were scored by the opponent being guarded?
7. Did player recover a loose ball?
8. Did player make a bad pass?
9. Did player fumble the ball?
10. Did player tire easily?
11. Did player argue with the officials?

Some teams go even farther. A team manager may have extra sheets with diagrams of the playing court printed on them. On these diagrams coaches and team managers indicate the plays used by the opponents, marking the spot where they occurred.

Studying the Records

All the record-keeping is put to good use. Teams need the information that is gathered so that they can know their own strong and weak points and also all about the playing ability of their rival teams.

The coach posts the team and player records

on a bulletin board. This gives the players a chance to study their own playing skills. Team members can see how well they scored, guarded, passed the ball, and everything else they did on the court during the game.

Most important of all, the coach and the team can see what skills must be practiced in order to improve their game. It's what the team does after studying the records that counts. That's what makes some teams the league champions.

Souvenir Programs

Basketball programs are not sold or distributed at many games because the official scoreboard gives a great deal of information. However, souvenir programs are usually sold at championship games. These programs give the starting line-up, players' positions, and list of substitutes for the game.

There is also other interesting information on these programs, such as team records, players' records, and each player's height, weight, age, and home town.

Figuring Percentages

The real sports fan likes to study team percentages. A great deal of work goes on behind the scenes to compile these figures. Many workers figure these percentages, which give us much information about the games.

Some percentage figures show the player and team standings in each league. These figures tell the fans:
1. The team's standing in the league.
2. The team's offensive and defensive averages.
3. Each player's field-goal percentage.
4. Each player's free-throw percentage.
5. Each player's fouling average.

If you know how to do percentage problems, it is fun to check and see if the figures are correct.

Team Percentage

To figure the team percentage or "team standing" in the league, take the number of games won and divide by the number of games played. The answers should be carried out to three places.

Example: The Panthers played ten games. They won seven games and lost three. What is the Panther's percentage, or standing, in the league?

$$10\overline{)7.000} = .700$$ *Panther's team percentage in the league*

Player's Scoring Average

To figure a player's scoring average for each game, take the total number of points scored for all the games played and divide by the number of games. Carry this answer out to one place.

Example: Bobby scored ninety-eight points in eight games. What was his scoring average per game?

$$8\overline{)98.0} \quad 12.2 \text{ points}$$ *Bobby's scoring average per game*

Sample Score Sheet

Here is one of the many different kinds of scoresheets used by a team.

KEY TO FIGURES
(*numbers marked with a line*):

No. Quarters: shows the quarters each member played.
Number: shows each player's number.
Personal Fouls: shows the number of personal fouls each member made.
Running Score: line drawn through the last number shows the final score of the game.
Quarters: shows scores made in each quarter.

SYMBOLS FOR SCORES:
Every figure 2 stands for a field goal scored in that quarter.

PANTHERS : BOY—GIRL TEAM

No. Quarters	Number	NAME	Personal Fouls	Quarter 1	Quarter 2	Quarter 3	Quarter 4	Running Score
1̶ 2̶ 3 4	5	Harvie	1̶ 2̶ 3 4 5 6	2-0-⊗		⊗-2-2		6̶1̶ 6̶2̶ 6̶3̶ 64 6̶5̶ 6̶6̶ 6̶7̶ 6̶8̶ 6̶9̶ 70 7̶1̶ 7̶2̶ 7̶3̶ 74 75 76 7̶7̶ 78 79 80 8̶1̶ 8̶2̶ 8̶3̶ 8̶4̶ 8̶5̶ 8̶6̶ 8̶7̶ 8̶8̶ 89 90 9̶1̶ 9̶2̶ 93 9̶4̶ 9̶5̶ 96 97 9̶8̶ 99 100 101 102 103 104 105 106 107 108 109 110 111 112 113 114 115 116 117 118 119 120
1 2̶ 3̶ 4̶	7	Bobby	1̶ 2̶ 3 4 5 6	⊗-2-2	2-0		0-2	
1 2̶ 3 4̶	11	Jimmy	1̶ 2 3 4̶ 5 6̶		2-0		⊗	
1 2̶ 3̶ 4̶	3	Criss	1 2 3 4̶ 5̶ 6			0-2	0	
1̶ 2̶ 3̶ 4̶	1	Tony	1̶ 2̶ 3 4 5 6	2-⊗	0		⊗	
1̶ 2̶ 3 4	9	Barbie	1̶ 2̶ 3 4 5 6	2	0			
1 2̶ 3 4̶	13	Eddie	1̶ 2̶ 3 4 5 6		⊗	0		
1̶ 2̶ 3̶ 4̶	15	Jack	1̶ 2̶ 3 4 5̶ 6	2			2-0	
1 2̶ 3 4̶	17	Amy	1̶ 2̶ 3 4 5 6		2-⊗	2		
		TOTALS BY QUARTERS		**15**	**8**	**9**	**6**	**FINAL 38**

TIME OUT ①②③④

Every figure ○ shows the number of free throws tried and missed.

Every figure ⊗ shows the number of free throws scored for one point.

Totals by Quarters: This shows the total score for each quarter.

Time Out: The circles around these numbers show the number of time-outs taken by the team.

Game Results

During the basketball season your newspaper prints a record of all games played every day. This record is known as "Game Results" and tells what happened on the playing court.

Team Standings

The newspapers also print the team standings of each conference, or league.

TEAM STANDINGS			
	W	L	Pct.
Panthers	9	2	.818
Wildcats	7	5	.583
Horsemen	6	5	.545
Warriors	6	5	.545
Beavers	6	6	.500
Vikings	6	6	.500
Troopers	6	6	.500
Bisons	5	6	.455
Trojans	5	6	.455
Eagles	1	10	.091

YESTERDAY'S RESULTS
Panthers 76 Wildcats 70
Horsemen 71 Eagles 69
Trojans 78 Vikings 62
Beavers 81 Warriors 78
Troopers 69 Bisons 68

GAMES TODAY
Panthers at Bisons
Warriors at Horsemen
Trojans at Beavers
Eagles at Vikings
Troopers at Wildcats

Key to figures:
W games won
L games lost
Pct. percentage of games won.

Voting for the Top Teams

All through the season the newspaper sportswriters and leading coaches throughout the country keep their eyes on the outstanding

GAME RESULTS

PANTHERS (77)	G-ST	F-FT	R	A	P	Pts.	WILDCATS (65)	G-ST	F-FT	R	A	P	Pts.
Don	9— 6	7—7	8	1	3	24	Steve	5— 1	4—7	13	2	2	14
José	4—13	5—6	10	3	5	13	Nick	1— 2	0—0	1	0	2	2
Jerry	3— 8	1—2	9	3	3	7	Sol	5— 8	5—6	5	0	5	15
Len	0— 2	0—0	1	6	0	0	Wally	3— 9	4—5	5	7	3	10
Burl	12—14	1—0	1	4	2	25	Jimmy	1— 3	0—0	1	0	0	2
Johnny	2— 8	0—0	0	8	1	4	Danny	3— 7	0—1	1	1	3	6
Alfredo	0— 2	0—0	0	2	0	0	Juan	1— 2	0—0	1	0	3	2
Stan	0— 0	4—4	3	1	2	4	Eddie	7— 8	0—0	1	3	1	14
Fred	0— 2	0—0	0	0	0	0	Art	0— 0	0—0	1	0	0	0
Totals	30 55	18 19	32	28	16	77		26 50	13 19	29	13	19	65

Team Score by Quarters

Panthers	21	18	17	21	-77
Wildcats	22	15	15	12	-65

Key to figures: number after team name is total score.

G means goals made by player. ST means shots taken at goal. F means fouls (free throws) made. FT means foul shots tried. R means rebounds. A means assists. P means personal fouls made by player. Totals are shown at the bottom of each column.

Basketball's Top Teams

MEN					WOMEN				
		W	L	Pts.			W	L	Pts.
Panthers	(20)	14	1	981	Owls	(22)	15	1	792
Raiders	(16)	14	1	972	Bruins	(19)	15	1	738
Wildcats	(17)	15	2	760	Hoosiers	(16)	14	2	698
Hornets	(11)	16	1	665	Bears	(11)	14	2	662
Lions	(3)	11	3	663	Gators	(5)	13	2	624
Horsemen	(3)	13	2	575	Longhorns	(4)	12	1	584
Hawks	(1)	14	3	566	Violets	(3)	11	1	543
Cardinals	(1)	15	3	420	Queens	(3)	13	3	495
Eagles	(2)	13	2	411	Naiads	(1)	12	3	440
Tigers	(1)	14	4	354	Rebels	(1)	14	4	390

Key to figures:
Figure after team means total number of first-place votes received.
W means number of games won.
L means number of games lost.
Pts. means total number of points received from votes.

Player Statistics
Leading Scorers (Men's Teams)

	G	F.G.	F.T.	PTS.	AVG.
1. Harvey, Wildcats	46	533	231	1297	28.2
2. Bobby, Panthers	47	490	289	1269	27.0
3. Jorge, Cardinals	45	447	300	1194	26.5
4. Joe, Horsemen	47	472	261	1205	25.6
5. Chuck, Troopers	41	415	206	1036	25.3
6. Al, Hornets	45	445	245	1135	25.2
7. Merrill, Raiders	47	488	177	1153	24.5
8. Tony, Vikings	44	402	266	1070	24.3
9. Henry, Beavers	44	415	240	1070	24.3
10. Wally, Lions	47	440	212	1092	23.2

Key to figures:
G number of games played.
F.G. field goals scored.
F.T. free throws scored.
Pts. total number of points scored.
Avg. average number of points per game.

teams. Then, at the end of the season, a committee of sportswriters and coaches vote to determine the top teams in each league and also in the whole country. The team that receives the highest number of points is rated as the *top team*.

Of course, the newspapers also report the playing statistics of the leading women scorers.

More Newspaper and Magazine Records

At the end of the season, newspapers and magazines list many more basketball records. Some of these show:
1. The best teams on offense.
2. The best teams on defense.
3. The best players in free-throw percentages.

All these records tell a story. They make interesting reading and keep the game alive long after the playing season is over. Sports fans like to study these figures and then try to predict next year's winners.

Rebounding

	G	Off.	Def.	Tot.	Avg.
Sally	48	177	606	783	16.3
Mary	42	143	493	636	15.1
Kathleen	47	293	398	691	14.7
Rita	48	182	453	653	13.6
Celeste	44	96	498	594	13.5

Key to figures:
G. number games played
Off. rebounds on offense
Def. rebounds on defense
Tot. total rebounds
Avg. average number rebounds per game

Assists

	G	No.	Avg.
Anne	48	469	9.8
Maria	47	459	9.8
Marlene	45	330	7.3
Lucy	46	333	7.2
Helga	46	311	6.8

Key to figures:
G games played
No. number assists made
Avg. number assists per game

Boys' and girls' teams figure out their records in the same way.

If you enjoy arithmetic and would like to do some extra problems, work out your own percentages and see how well you played during the season. This means that you should keep an accurate account of your game and the scores you made. After every game, write them down in your basketball notebook. Work out your percentages and keep them up to date. Then, at the end of the season, you will have your own personal records, just like the leading players in the country.

Chapter 13

Everyone Can Play Basketball

It is wise to have a physical checkup before taking part in active sports. If you find that you should not play, do not be discouraged. Many people cannot play with their school or neighborhood teams.

There was a man who never played a game of basketball in his life. But that didn't stop him from enjoying the game. In fact, he became a winning coach, and his team won the state high-school basketball championship!

You can work with your team and enjoy the game, too. These suggestions may help you choose what you may do.

Serve on the Game Committee. Help arrange

for games. Find the proper teams to play against.

Be a Team Secretary. Keep the scores and records for your team.

Be the Team Treasurer. Take care of the money used by the club.

Help the Coach. The coach invents new plays and makes diagrams of them. Print these forms on an office machine for the team to study.

Help the Game Officials. Be an assistant scorekeeper or timer.

Sell Tickets. Ticket selling is an important way of helping the team pay expenses.

Be an Usher. Show the fans to their seats and be able to answer questions about the team and players.

Do Publicity Work.
1. Advertise the games. Write news items telling when and where the games will take place. Send these news items to your school and community newspapers.
2. Send these notices to the TV and radio stations.
3. Make signs and posters. If you like to draw and can do neat lettering, make signs and posters telling about the games. Place them in the school corridors, public library, and neighborhood stores.

Be a Sportswriter. After a game, write it up for your school and city papers. Tell the scores and give the highlights of the game.

Make Up Cheers and Drills.
1. Make up cheers that are new and different.
2. Work out interesting drills using white or colored cards or small flags.

All these things add to the fun and excitement of the game and they also inspire the team to play its best.

Perhaps your doctor may allow you to do some light practicing. If you get approval, try these exercises:

Shoot for baskets. Try some free throws, chest shots, and overhead shots.

Help your team practice.
1. Rebound Drills
   Shoot baskets and the players will try to recover the ball on a rebound.
2. Passing drills
   Toss the ball to a player who will shoot for the basket.
   Bounce the ball to a player who will charge down the court with a fast dribble.
   Roll the ball to a teammate who will pick it up and continue with the next play.

Do not run or jump while doing these exercises. Do not practice for too long a time!

Discuss this list of suggestions with your parents and doctor.

Wheelchair Basketball

Wheelchair basketball is played by people young and old. Teams are organized in schools, colleges, and neighborhood clubs.

The wheelchair game has spread to countries all over the world. These teams even have end-of-season tournament games to find the winners.

First Tournament and Olympic Competition

The first wheelchair basketball tournament was organized in 1949 at the University of Illinois. This led to the formation of the *National Wheelchair Basketball Association.* The game became so popular that other countries soon adopted a form of the wheelchair game. Teams from the United States began to enter international competition. The year 1960 marked the first time that wheelchair basketball was held in connection with the regular World Olympic Games.

Immediately following the regular Olympic Games, competition wheelchair athletes from all over the world assembled in Rome and held their first international contest, known as the *Para-Olympics* (Olympics for paraplegics).

Wheelchair Basketball Rules

A form of wheelchair basketball may be played by young people who use wheelchairs to get about. You must have the permission of your doctor before playing. These games should be played under the direction of a coach, teacher, or parent.

Most wheelchair basketball leagues follow the rules of regular basketball with only the following major changes:
1. In dribbling, a player may not push more than twice in succession on the wheelchair handrims in any direction before tapping the ball to the floor, shooting, or passing. Three pushes count as a "traveling with ball" violation.
2. An offensive player is allowed six seconds in the free-throw lane, while in regular basketball only three seconds are allowed.
3. Players may not raise themselves off the seat of their chairs. If the rule is broken, a "physical advantage foul" is called and will be treated as a technical foul, but with no free throw awarded.
4. Three physical advantage fouls against a player mean expulsion from the game.

Basketball for Mentally Retarded

Did you know that there are active programs for youngsters who are slow or retarded mentally?

One popular organization promoting basketball for the mentally slow is the *Joseph P. Kennedy Jr. Foundation.* It is named after the brother of former President John F. Kennedy.

Mentally slow, retarded, or handicapped boys and girls from age 8 to 18 can qualify for one of the many *Special Sports and Fitness Awards* offered by the Kennedy Foundation.

Check with your school, club, parents' organization, camp, or playground instructor for information.

If you want extra basketball competition, the foundation sponsors a *Special Olympics* for the mentally slow. Boys and girls aged 8 years and over are eligible. You have a choice of taking part in basketball, physical fitness, and many more events.

Whether you are physically handicapped or mentally slow, you have an opportunity to get active in your favorite program.

Who knows? With daily hard work and the good care of your body, you may discover fitness and basketball skills you never knew you had. So, work hard to strengthen your mind and body.

WHEELCHAIR PRACTICE DRILLS

Young wheelchair players must practice the skills, too.

1. Wheel over to the free-throw line. Practice these shots:
    a. Two-hand chest shot
    b. Two-hand overhead shot
    c. One-hand push shot

See how many baskets you can make out of ten tries for each of the shots. Your teacher or a teammate assistant will toss the ball back to you after each shot.

2. Two wheelchair players face each other about 5 yards apart.
    a. Practice throwing the ball back and forth

MAKING A PASS

SCRAMBLE FOR BALL

to each other. This is a good exercise in passing and receiving.
    b. As you improve in handling the ball, move the wheelchairs farther apart and increase the throwing distance.
    c. Try these passes while the receiver is moving. This means that your receiver is on the move with his/her wheelchair as you toss the ball to him/her.
3. Wall-target Practice.
    a. If you don't have a basketball backboard, make a wall target. You can draw a target on the wall with chalk or paint. Or a cloth target can be attached to the wall.
    b. Try the different shots at the wall target.
    c. Practice the different shots to a teammate who is not in a wheelchair. This player will toss the ball back to you.

Wheelchair Game Using One Basket

This game is for two teams with two or more players on each team. It is played on one half of the court and only one basket is used. The idea of the game is to see which side can shoot the most baskets and pile up the highest score.

Rules of the Game

1. A player with the ball may move anywhere on the court until it is the right moment to shoot for the basket.

2. A player cannot hold the ball longer than fifteen seconds.
3. A player is warned when s/he gets closer than 3 feet to an opposing player who has the ball.
4. It is a foul if a player's wheelchair touches the wheelchair of the opponent with the ball.
5. If a shot to the basket is missed, the opposing team takes the ball for a throw-in.
6. If a pass is not caught, the ball goes to the opposing team.

The rules of the game may be changed from time to time. However, the teacher or coach must get the doctor's permission before making any changes.

If it is not possible for you to take part in any of these activities, there are other ways to enjoy the game. You can go to see the games, watch them on television, or listen to them over the radio.

It's interesting to read about the games in the sports section of the newspapers. There are some fine sports magazines, too. Go to the library and load up on sports books. Become the expert speaker and writer about the game.

Best of all you can discuss the games with your friends. It's always fun to talk about sports. So, whether or not you take some part in the team activities, it's exciting to be a loyal team fan or worker.

Chapter 14

Dribble It!
Pass It!
Shoot It!

The basketball season is over. The All-American teams have been chosen. School, club, and playground championships have been won. Still, the game goes on!

Factory and office workers, doctors, lawyers, laborers, and boys and girls play basketball all year round. They play outdoors and indoors. They play wherever there are baskets.

All over the country you can see baskets attached over garage doors, barns, and on posts. People, old and young, love to shoot baskets. They play from the end of one season until another season starts.

Listen! There goes the referee's whistle. Two tall centers stand in the jump circle ready for the tip-off. The fans cheer.

Another season begins. This game, which was born in the United States of America and started with two peach baskets, keeps going all year. Basketball is fun for everyone. Get into the game!

Index

All-American, 11–12
All-Conference teams, 10–11
Arranging for games, 120

Backboards and baskets, 18, 122–123
Balls, early, 7, 11
  official, 126
Basketball tests 137–155
  AAHPER, 138–154
  dribble, 152–154
  foul shot, 143–144
  front shot, 140–141
  jump and reach, 146–148
  overarm pass for accuracy, 148–149
  push pass for accuracy, 149–151
  side shot, 142–143
  speed pass, 145–146
  under basket shot, 144–145
Biddy Basketball, age of players, 12
  championships, 12
  court, official measurements, 121–122
  field equipment, 122–124
  length of game, 17–18, 132–133
  personal equipment, 124–126
Bounce pass, 82–83
Boxer's shuffle, 37, 38
Boxing-out, 41–43

Catching ball, above-the-waist, 93, 94
  below-the-waist, 94, 95
  on-the-bounce, 97
  on-the-run, 96–97, 99

Catching, drills and hints, 98–99
  rolling ball, 97–98
  from a stationary position, 92, 93, 98
Championship games, 9–13
Chest pass, 78–80
Courts, Biddy Basketball, 18–19, 121–122
Courts, elementary,
  high school and college, 18–19
Crossing-under-basket shot, 72–73

Defense drills, 115–116
Defensive strategy, 102–107
  all-court press, 106
  boxing-out on the rebound, 107
  player-to-player defense, 102–103
  shifting player-to-player, 103–104
  zone defenses, 104–106
Dribble, change-of-hands, 52–53
  double, 55
  high, 51–52
  low, 48–50
Dribble, drills and hints, 56–58
  stances, 49, 51, 52
Dribble test, 152–154
Dribbling, 22, 47–58
  fake, 53–54, 110–111

Early, backboards and baskets, 4
  basketballs, 7, 11
  game rules, 5–6
  uniforms, 5, 7–8
Equipment, Biddy Basketball court, 122–124

earning money for, 127–129
Equipment, official ball, 126
officials, 126–127
young players' personal, 124–126

Fake, change-of-direction dribble, 54–55
pass, 88
shot and dribble, 53–54
Faking plays on offense, 109–112
Field goal, 20
Figuring percentage, 160–161
First basketball games, indoors, 2–4
outdoors, 8–9
Forwards, 16–17
Foul shot test, 143–144
Fouls, common, 20–21
technical, 21
Free throw, 20–21, 61–64
circle, 18, 122
lane, 18, 122
line, 18, 122
Front shot test, 140–141

Girls' Basketball, 6, 13
early games, 6
early uniforms, 5, 7–8
first olympics, 13
Globetrotters, 13–14
Guarding, a dribbler, 40–41
after shot at basket, 41
duties, 16–17, 33–35
for lay-up shot, 43, 44
offensive player with ball, 38–39
pivot player, 39–40
stance, 36–38
Guarding hints and drills, 43–46

Hand-off pass, 87–88
Held ball, 23
Hook, pass, 85–87
shot, 70–72

Illegal dribble, 22
Intercepted pass, 22

Jump and reach test, 146–148
Jump ball, 23

Jump circle, 18
Jump shot, one-hand, 69–70
two-hand, 73
Jump stop, 28–29
Jump-turn shot, 73–74

Kennedy, Foundation, Joseph P., 173–174
Key-lock, 122

Lay-up shot, 67–69
Length of game, 17–18, 132–33
Little Guys and Gals, championships, 12
rules, 135–136
Mentally retarded, basketball for, 10, 173–174

Naismith, Dr. James A., 4
National, Basketball Association, 13
championships, 11
Collegiate Basketball Association, 11
National Federation of State High School Associations, 121
National Wheelchair Basketball Association, 10, 171–173

Offense drills, 116–117
Offensive strategy, 107–115
fake plays, 109–115
fast-break, 109
pivot-plays and hand-offs, 112–115
slow-break, 108–109
Officials, 130–131
Officials' equipment, 126–127
Olympic Basketball tournaments, 10, 13
One-hand, jump shot, 69–70
set shot, 64–67
Out-of-bounds, 24
Overarm pass for accuracy test, 148–149
Overhead pass, 83–85

Pass, hand-off, 87–88
hook, 85–87
two-hand bounce, 82–83
two-hand chest, 78–80

Pass, two-hand overhead, 83–85
   two-hand underhand, 80–82
Passes, kinds of, 78
   fake, 88
Passing, different ways of, 22
   drills and hints, 88–89
Peach basket game, 2–4
Pivot, player, 39–40
   shot, 70–72
   step, 29–30
Players' records, 158
Playing court, official, 18–19
   Biddy Basketball, 18–19, 121–122
Points in scoring, 20–21
Professional basketball teams, 13–14
Programs, 160
Push pass for accuracy test, 149–151

Records, team, 157–158
   player, 158
Referee, 126, 130

Scorekeeper, 130, 157, 158
Scorekeeping, 156–168
Scoring, 18
Scoresheets, 162–164
Set shots, 60–61
   free throw, 61–64
   one-hand, 64–67
   two-hand, 60–64
Shooting drills, 74–76
Shots used in games, 60
Side shot for accuracy test, 142–143
Signals used by officials, 24
Special Olympics, 10, 174
Speed pass test, 145–146
Stance, above-the-waist catch, 93–94
   below-the-waist catch, 94–95
   change-of-hands dribble, 52–53
Stance for all-purpose players, 26–27
Stance, guarding, 36–38
   high-dribble, 51–52
   low-dribble, 48–50
   two-hand set shot, 60–64

Strategy, defensive, 102–107
   drills, 115–116
   plays, 16–17, 102–107
Strategy, offensive, 107–115
   drills, 116–117
   plays, 16–17
Substitutes, 23

Team, helpers, 169–171
   records, 157–158
   uniforms, 124–126
Teamwork, 101–102
Technical foul, 21
Tests. *See* basketball tests
Three-two zone defense, 105, 106
Timekeeper, 131
Time-outs, 23
Tip-in shot, 72
Tournaments, 9–10
Training rules, 118–119
Traveling with the ball, 24
Two-hand, bounce pass, 82–83
   chest pass, 78–80
   jump shot, 73
   set shot, 60–64
   underhand pass, 81–82
Two-one-two zone defense, 104, 105
Two-three zone defense, 104, 105

Umpire, 126, 130
Under basket shot test, 144–145
Underhand pass, 81–82

Wheelchair Basketball, 10, 171–173, 174–177
Women's early basketball uniform, 5, 7–8
World Olympic Games, 10, 13

Y M C A Training School, 8
Youth Basketball Association 12, 121
   age of players, 132
   length of game, 132–133
   rules, 132, 133, 134

About the Authors

ROBERT J. ANTONACCI, Ed. D., has been associated with sports and fitness all his life. A professor at Temple University, Philadelphia, he is a former national champion, a coach of college champions, and author of a number of textbooks. Dr. Antonacci is in demand as a lecturer and demonstrator of how sports and fitness books for young people can stimulate improvements in reading, mathematics, spelling, physics, and other subjects. With Jene Barr he has written YOUNG CHAMPION books on baseball, football, and physical fitness; he co-authored TRACK AND FIELD FOR YOUNG CHAMPIONS with Gene Schoor; and SOCCER FOR YOUNG CHAMPIONS with Tony Puglisi. Dr. Antonacci is now at work on a tennis book.

JENE BARR has been a physical-education teacher, an elementary-school teacher, and a librarian in the Chicago public schools. Her books for children number more than twenty, and have earned her the Midwest Award of the Children's Reading Round Table. She also won first prize from the Illinois Women's Press Association for a popular children's newspaper column. She is the co-author of four books in the YOUNG CHAMPION series. Jene Barr now lives in Sunnyvale, California.

j796.323
Antonacci, R
  Basketball for young champions
2nd ed.

MAR 20

State of Vermont
Department of Libraries
Midstate Regional Library
RFD #4
Montpelier, Vt. 05602

WITHDRAWN

VERMONT DEPT. OF LIBRARIES
0 00 01 0286557 3